SWIM LIKE A PRO

Edited and formatted by L. Austen Johnson

SWIM LIKE A PRO BONUS VIDEO COURSE

I truly believe that the best way to learn something is through multiple touch points. That's why I created an online video course that corresponds with this book.

I have created a unique video for each chapter that will aid in your learning. You'll be able to see and hear my explanation for each concept and stroke technique in this book. Seeing a visual representation of each concept can make all the difference in how fast you make progress, so I highly recommend you join the online course.

You can get started right away by visiting swimlikeapro.org or by opening the camera app on your phone. Hold your phone over the QR code below. Your phone will automatically direct you to the website where you can follow the instructions to unlock all the video content.

ONLINE COURSE

SCAN THE CODE

TO SWIM LIKE A PRO

VIDEO LIBRARY

WORKOUTS

Q&A

PREFACE

A Love Letter To Swimming

THE FEELING OF WEIGHTLESSNESS is unlike anything I've experienced in my life. When I'm swimming, it feels like I've entered a different world. It's as if I've been transported to another dimension. The world's problems just disappear, and I become one with the water.

It's Magical.

When I first dive in, all my senses awaken, and I experience something that transcends imagination. The water tingles along my skin, bringing my senses to life. I hear the molecules of water echoing inside my eardrum as I submerge below the surface. I can smell the water, fresh and natural, and even get a little taste with my lips.

It's truly a one-of-a-kind experience, and nothing else will engage all my senses like the feeling of being in water. After all, we as humans are 60% water, so it's a bit like coming home. But there's something more to this experience than becoming one with the water, a medium that covers most of the world's surface area. There's something about the feeling of weightlessness that is special, and it is this feeling that is one of the many joys the sport of swimming offers humanity.

Think of your body as a vessel. When you start to swim, every part of your body works together to move your vessel forward. Some body parts and energy systems work harder than others. Your heart beats faster to pump blood to your muscles, while your stomach slows down because digestion is no longer a priority.

After about two minutes, your body realizes that you're not stopping anytime soon and goes into aerobic respiration. Your body starts to supply even more oxygen to your muscles. Your heart beats faster and stronger to circulate this oxygenated blood through your body!

Our brains love swimming too! The extra blood and oxygen circulating help you become more alert, awake, and focused. When we swim, our brain releases endorphins, natural, "feel good" hormones. When you swim, your mind can be just as engaged as your body, and as a result, your future self will thank you.

There is no question that swimming is the best all-around form of physical fitness for all. It's the only form of physical activity that you can do from cradle to grave. The water has no racial, national, or religious boundaries. Young, old, rich, poor, from anywhere around the world, we are all working towards the same goals.

Together we share a passion for the water. Whether you swim for sport, physical fitness, or mental health, whether you swim in a pool, lake, river, the sea, or the ocean, we are all in this together!

It's that feeling of weightlessness, competitive spirit, and pushing ourselves further and faster! It's the positive endorphins we feel after reaching the wall, crossing the finish line, or looking in the mirror knowing you're a badass for diving in and taking on the world!

This is why I swim!

Since my early childhood, I developed a great passion for the water. The freedom and enjoyment we experience as swimmers is often hard to describe. My experience in the water has empowered me to help others realize this same feeling of freedom.

I believe through structured guidance, data, and social interaction, we are all just one day away from realizing our full potential! Aquatic prowess is the epiphany of reaching your full potential in the water.

In 2015, I launched MySwimPro, a fitness app to help swimmers all over the world improve their performance and health. The idea for the app was to have a personalized swim coaching experience at a fraction of the cost of hiring a coach. MySwimPro has grown to over one million community members. Our mission is to democratize swimming by making improvement easier and more accessible to all swimmers.

Through the development of this global swimming business, I've had the opportunity to speak with thousands of swimmers around the world about their goals, fears, and dreams in the sport. I've interviewed dozens of olympians, world record holders, and industry experts on everything from strength training to nutrition.

I've written thousands of personalized workouts and training plans for swimmers with highly diverse backgrounds and goals. The results are absolutely incredible! From helping people lose over 100lbs to crossing the finish line at their very first triathlon, the impact has been palpable.

Before launching MySwimPro, I coached both age-group and masters swimmers. I truly enjoyed the opportunity to help people improve their techniques and reach their goals. After the 2016 Olympic Trials, I transitioned to coaching only masters swimmers to allocate more time to growing MySwimPro. It's an amazing experience to share the knowledge I have gained as a former collegiate swimmer with people of all skills and experience levels.

As a swimmer myself, I still compete in masters competitions, open water races, and in triathlons. I've competed in the FINA Masters World Championships, swam from Asia to Europe in the Bosphorus Cross Continental swim, and am a 3x U.S. Masters swimming individual national champion. I'm always on the lookout for the next swimming adventure, and in this book, I'll tie in relevant stories for added flavor and entertainment.

This book is the culmination of over a decade of on-deck coaching experience, 20+ years competitive swimming knowledge, and over five years building the largest digital swimming community in the world!

I am incredibly excited to package all this knowledge into one book that takes a holistic approach to helping swimmers reach their goals. Please also visit swimlikeapro.org for this book's special online companion course that is filled with instructional technique videos and other resources to help you swim smarter.

This is THE most comprehensive way to swim faster and smarter than ever before. There is only one question I have for you:

Are you ready to swim like a pro?

CONTENTS

Part Three

MAIN SET II:

Out of the Water

Part Four

COOL DOWN:

Swim for life

Part Five

APPENDICES

INTRODUCTION

You feel it the moment you enter the water. Your heart pounds, your muscles contract, and your lungs tighten up! A few minutes later, you've moved beyond the initial temperature shock and floated into a world where swimming is almost as comfortable as walking.

Throughout this book, I'll share a methodology that has been used by thousands of swimmers around the world to improve stroke technique and swim more efficiently. I'll walk you through a holistic approach that will allow you to swim with less effort, swim faster, and swim with more enjoyment than ever before.

If you're just getting started in your swimming journey, this couldn't be a better time to start! The resources I'll share in this book and the online course will not only expose you to the fundamentals of technique training but also the world of strength and conditioning, nutrition, and injury prevention.

Before we get started, I'd like to share with you the five core promises of this book and my intentions behind them. Each promise is my commitment to you. If you approach this book and the methodology I share with an open mind, you will be in a significantly better position to take your swimming to the next level.

PROMISE #1: A FRESH PERSPECTIVE ON SWIMMING

Albert Einstein is widely credited with saying, "The definition of insanity is doing the same thing over and over again but expecting different results." If you want to maximize your potential in something, you must approach it with a fresh perspective. Whether you've been swimming for 30 years or just getting started, I promise that this book will help expand your outlook on every aspect of swimming. We will start by self-reflecting on why you swim and how to prioritize your goals and create a plan of action to reach them!

PROMISE #2: A DEEPER UNDERSTANDING OF STROKE TECHNIQUE AND TRAINING

Water is 784 times more dense than air! It is a medium that offers its own unique physical challenges unlike anything we experience on land. For this reason, we must take a scientific approach to understanding the physics of how our body moves through the water. I promise to present to you a detailed technical overview of all five strokes: freestyle, backstroke, breaststroke, butterfly, and the underwater dolphin kick. Additionally, I will share workouts and video demonstrations in the complementary online course.

PROMISE #3: A STRATEGY TO SET SMART GOALS

A goal without a plan is just a wish. If you make a wish to Santa to swim faster, he may or may not deliver. You should still leave him milk and cookies just in case. In this book, I promise to share drills, training guidance, and a strategy to build on the technical knowledge for each stroke we discuss. You will learn how to set SMART Goals that are specific, measurable, attainable, and time-bound. You will put together an action plan and join a global community of swimmers who are focused on improving their performance and health!

PROMISE #4: A HOLISTIC APPROACH TO SWIM SMARTER

If you want to swim faster, you have to swim more. This is false. Instead, I will share how to swim smarter and incorporate both in-water and out-of-water training to enhance your performance and make the most of your time. We will discuss how these elements come together and why it matters if you're looking to take your swimming to the next level!

PROMISE #5: TO BE INSPIRED

We all have our own unique motivations to swim. Perhaps you're looking to reach a personal best time, or maybe, you aspire to swim in an open water race or triathlon. Maybe you're looking to improve your stroke technique and burn more calories. Regardless of your goal, you're not alone. Swimming is special. We have a global community of individuals who have achieved incredible progress and made strides to what I like to call "Gold Medal Moments."

You don't have to win gold to achieve something great! In this book and supplemental video interviews, you will hear from people just like yourself who are working towards their personal goals and finding success. I believe that we are all just one step away from achieving our Gold Medal Moment. We just need the right guidance, structure, and support to make it happen.

I can't promise you'll break a world record or hit a new PR, but with the resources presented in this book and online course content, you'll be well on your way to swimming with more efficiency and greater confidence in the water.

So how will we do this?

A Holistic Approach

I want you to think about your favorite high performance sports car. Maybe you like exotic Italian supercars like Lamborghini or Bugatti. Perhaps you're a fan of classic American Muscle cars or new age electric. Regardless if you fancy a Ferrari or a Tesla, all these automobiles have one thing in common.

They've all been engineered to be the best at something while still being great at everything else. Similarly, the best swimmers in the world share the same fundamentals of stroke technique, training, and race strategy. The best swimmers approach swimming from a holistic perspective in order to optimize every element of the human machine. Fast cars and fast swimmers have a lot more in common than you might think.

At the core of a car's performance is the engine. An internal machine that converts one form of energy into another for forward motion. When it comes to swimming, we have the unique opportunity to train and develop our engines. We can even make our engines more efficient to improve our range. Instead of fuel economy, we have something called swimming economy, i.e., how efficient we are at swimming. Remember, we are a vessel moving through the water. What good is a powerful engine if it's not working efficiently?

The fastest cars also have the least wind resistance. Similarly, as a swimmer, it's our job to decrease drag and limit our resistance with the water. Unlike a car moving through air, we move through water, a medium that's 800x denser than air.

When it comes to stabilizing the machine, just like a performance car, you can't load a massive engine on a weak frame.

Similarly, we as swimmers must have a strong core to hold our alignment in the water and support forward progress.

Just like a car, some features are essential; others are not. The shiny rims, heated seats, and carbon fiber accents are cosmetic features that might be flashy, but at the end of the day, they're simply just nice to have. In swimming, you can think of these cosmetic features as your swimsuit color, cap, goggles, and equipment.

There are so many possibilities to customize, but the core of the machine is what's on the inside. For the car, that's the engine, transmission, chasis, and internal computer system. For swimmers, this would be our stroke technique, endurance, and knowledge of the sport.

By the end of this book, you'll have the knowledge and know-how to go on auto-pilot. But I don't recommend swimming on autopilot. After all, the fun of driving a car is being in the driver seat, and swimming is no different!

When you're in the driver's seat, you're in control. Let's rev our engines because this joy ride is about to start!

Book Structure

This book is broken up into four core sections that flow from one to the other. We'll start with the fundamentals of swimming by discussing the physics of how to swim faster and how to structure a workout. Then, we'll dive (pun intended) into each major stroke with a full overview of the proper mechanics. Each chapter in this section will share the proper technique for the corresponding stroke along with supplemental online content that will feature instructional video drills.

In the second half of the book, we'll step out of the water to teach skills that will supplement your swimming training. We'll look at how to approach swimming as a lifelong sport. I'll share goal setting strategies, how to get started, and personal stories from my swimming adventures around the world.

ARE YOU READY TO SWIM LIKE A PRO?

Let's dive in :)

WARMUP:

The Fundamentals

CHAPTER ONE

What Happens to Your Body When You Swim

WE AS HUMANS have five basic senses: touch, sight, hearing, smell and taste. Different parts of our body and the sensing organs associated with each sense (like our tongues, for example) send information to the brain to help us understand and perceive the world around us. In the water, we have a sixth sense.

Yes, we all have a sixth sense, and I'm not talking about the 1999 thriller movie starring Bruce Willis. Our sixth sense has more to do with body awareness and our "feel" of the water. This feeling of connection with the water is different than our sense of touch.

If you've been swimming for any consistent period of time, then you've probably already developed a love-hate relationship with your feel of the water. If you're new to swimming, this is your opportunity to start this relationship off on the right foot!

This is important because when we understand how our feel

of the water develops, we will have better insight into how to improve it. Having a greater awareness of your touch, sight, hearing, smell, taste, and feel of the water heightens your swimming experience. When you swim with all your senses, you improve most quickly, swim more efficiently, and you feel more alive!

Finding your Swimming Zen

I'm not a Zen monk, nor do I plan to become one. However, we can learn and gain insight in the way monks try to live their lives. Simplicity, mindfulness, calm, peace. These are all principles we can learn from.

We can all learn to make our swimming more Zen-like by following a few simple guidelines. One of these principles is simplicity–to do one thing at a time. Do one thing, and do it slowly and deliberately. Do it completely.

In life, we often overwhelm ourselves with more than we can handle. In swimming, unfortunately, we behave in a similar manner. There's so many things to think about in the water. Push off in streamline, point your toes, blow bubbles out of your nose, keep your core tight, take a break out stroke, don't let your hips drop.

There are literally hundreds of small movements and decisions that you can think about just from pushing off the wall and taking your first stroke. Regardless of how many things you could be focusing on, the key to improving is to simplify and focus on one skill at a time. In this book and online course, you will read about and see hundreds of different techniques, drills, and strategies.

If you try to apply all these skills at one time, you will most surely become frustrated and give up. It's important to take a systematic approach. Lead with simplicity. Do less, space it out, designate time for mastering certain skills, and think about what has the highest impact for you.

In order to find your swimming zen, it's important to keep everything in perspective and go with the flow. Remember, the water is 800x denser than air. You can't fight the water; you will surely lose. Instead, be patient, stay positive, and try your best to enjoy the feeling of weightlessness.

"The water is your friend.....you don't have to fight with water, just share the same spirit as the water, and it will help you move." - Alexandr Popov

SWIMMING ZEN DRILL:

The next time you go to the pool, try this fun and simple drill. I'd like you to enter the water feet first, fully submerge yourself so your entire body has had a chance to get wet, including your head.

Next, I want you to focus on relaxing your body by focusing on lowering your heart rate.

Focus on your breathing. Breathe in your nose, out your mouth. Don't hyperventilate, just breathe normally and calm your body. Think of this as a meditative exercise to clear your mind. Then when you're ready, drop your face in the water and float on your stomach. Let your arms float where they're most comfortable, and try to get your chest and hips high in the water.

You may want to inform the lifeguard what you're doing so

they don't look over and have a panic attack when they see you floating on your stomach in the shallow end! Assuming you're able to float for a few seconds, try to relax your body, clear your mind, and find your swimming zen.

> "The mind is like water. When it's turbulent, it's difficult to see. When it's calm, everything becomes clear." - Prasad Mahes

Body Awareness

Body awareness is the ability to recognize where your body is in space. This could be on land or in the water. In the swimming world, a strong sense of body awareness allows someone to time their final stroke into the wall at the finish of a race or figure out at what point to somersault on the wall for a freestyle flip turn.

Your muscles and joints send your brain information about your body and how it moves through the water. You may wonder why good body awareness is important to swimming fast. Body awareness helps us to understand how to connect our body to the water.

It's pretty easy to spot the level of a swimmer's body awareness at the pool. A beginner swimmer might take unnecessary strokes very close to the wall or have an irregular breathing pattern. Both of these traits are very common, and if this is you, no worries at all. We can change that by improving our body awareness in the water.

Even for more advanced swimmers, improving body awareness can help you swim faster, get a better more effective workout, and enjoy the sport more. Body awareness develops quickly throughout childhood development because research indicates that the multi-sensory foundations of the body develop throughout early and mid-childhood.

If you learned how to swim as a teenager or adult, you can still learn and develop these skills, it just takes time. The more time you spend in the water, the more you'll improve. So remember to be patient and focus on finding your swimming zen!

Be one with the water!

Proprioception

Proprioception is the body's mysterious ability to locate our limbs, in the water or even in darkness. You could call it body sense or kinesthetic awareness; it is the brain's ability to sense the relative positions and movements of our different body parts. Because of proprioception, you know exactly where your hand is in space as you move it around, even though your eyes are closed.

You can test your own proprioception to see how this works. Take this book or any object and hold it out in front of you with both hands. Now close your eyes. Continue holding the book out in front of you with one hand, and use your other hand to touch your nose. Now return your hand back to the book. Pretty easy, right?

Now let's make things a bit more challenging. Repeat this process of holding the book out in front of you and close your eyes. Touch your nose, now instead of returning your hand to the book, touch the back of your head and then give yourself a pat on the back. Now, without opening your eyes, try to return your hand to the top of the book where you started...

It's not as easy as you'd think. Good thing you patted yourself on the back first, because you probably missed returning your hand to the book. When we close our eyes, our sense of the world and our body's place in it doesn't disappear. An invisible impression remains. This sense is what proprioception is.

Like our other senses — vision, hearing, and so on — it helps our brains navigate the world. Scientists sometimes refer to it as our "sixth sense." As you could tell from the last activity, you may or may not have been successful at keeping your limbs in check while your eyes were closed.

This is because our brain maps our movements like the map of a road. When you travel the same path over and over, a new mind map is created. These maps are constantly being updated to reflect current demands. You can instantly sense changes in your maps by doing a simple experiment.

Try to imagine or sense the exact shape and position of your ears. Now, rub just the left ear for a few seconds and then compare your ability to sense the left ear and the right. You will note that it is much easier to sense the left. The simple reason is that touching the ear sent a signal to your brain, which activated the map for that area. Of course, the additional clarity is only temporary.

Similarly, when we swim, we create maps in our mind of how each stroke is supposed to work. Everything from the timing of how our fingertips enter the water to the way our muscles engage at each part of the stroke. We reinforce our own habits without even knowing it.

This is why it's so important to swim with proper stroke technique. Every stroke we take is an opportunity to refine and reinforce our mental framework for how to swim. In order to make long-term or permanent changes in the maps, you need to consistently place demands on that map over a long period of time.

For example, musicians actually have larger finger maps than other people. When a certain body part or movement is used repeatedly in a coordinated and mindful fashion, there are actual physical and observable changes in the part of the brain that controls that body part or movement.

This is part of the reason why you get better at what you practice. Lack of movement will reverse this process. If you fail to move in a certain way for a period of time, you lose the ability to accurately sense and control that movement. This is called sensory motor amnesia.

If we swim three to four times per week and then take an 8-week break from swimming, the brain's body map will become fuzzier and less clear. We'll feel as if we've "lost our feel of the water." There are ways to limit this impact and better maintain this feel of the water outside of the pool which we'll discuss in later chapters.

When it comes to improving our "feel of the water," we must be consistent in our approach. Developing our feel of the water takes time. It even has a compounding effect that's not linear. Each day we swim, and with each stroke we take, we refine our mind and body's connection with the water.

Out of the water, we can maintain and even accelerate these mind maps through functional dryland training. We'll go in detail on how we can do this in chapters nine and ten when we discuss swimming specific strength training and injury prevention.

Whether you're training in or out of the water, your rate of improvement starts with your intention. In order to re-calibrate your neural network so you can swim faster, you have to be willing to re-shape your approach. I advise looking at each new skill and workout with a fresh perspective.

You must engage both your mind and body in the water. Use all your senses to work together to help you reach your goals.

"The mind controls the body, and the mind is unlimited." - Craig Townsend

All Your Senses

When we're in the water, it's amazing how every muscle in our body is sending information to the brain at the same time. Our nervous system processes a massive amount of sensory data without any conscious work on our part.

Just think what it takes to push off the wall in streamline. All the muscles, from your fingertips to your toes, need to relay the right information at the right time so you can keep all the bones of your spine in line. Next, in order to start kicking in that position, you'll need to engage muscles in your core and legs at just the right timing to keep forward momentum. When you break streamline for the first stroke, your hand connects with the water in order to create forward propulsion for the rest of your body.

It's amazing what the brain is capable of. We've already discussed our "sixth sense," but we skipped over the core five that we're most familiar with, our senses of touch, sight, smell, hearing, and taste. All of these are important in swimming.

. . .

Touch

The average person has nearly 20 million skin cells on their body. When we go swimming, we get nearly 20 million interactions with the water all at the same time! That's insane!

If you ask anyone what sense is most engaged during physical activity, they would most likely say the sense of touch. I would agree! Our sense of touch is our primary connection to the water. It goes deeper than the surface (pun intended) of our skin, all the way to engagement on a neuromuscular level.

Sight

"The eyes are the window to your soul." - William Shakespeare

I think Shakespeare was trying to be deep with that quote, but in all reality, our eyes do offer us the opportunity to connect with the world around us. Our visual memory describes the relationship between our perception of what we see in the present moment and how it relates to what we've seen in the past.

If we imagine ourselves in the water, just think of everything we see and how it relates to our swimming—the transparency of the water, the depth of the bottom, where the backstroke flags are: There are so many visual cues we use to orient ourselves at the pool or in open water.

Smell

The next time you're at the pool or beach, pause and take in the scent of your environment. It may sound primitive, but it will open not just your nostrils but your mind, too. The sense of smell (called the "olfactory" sense) is closely linked with memory, probably more so than any of our other senses. The scent of chlorine conjures up recollections of a childhood summer swim team practice, for example.

Hearing

While our echoic memory only lasts 2-4 seconds, we immediately become aware of familiar sounds that we hear. Similarly to our sense of smell, our hearing is highly associated with long-term memory. Hearing the sounds of the ocean, a starting beep at a swimming competition, or even the sound we make when we push off the wall and blow bubbles out of our nose can all connect us to the water.

Taste

If you've been open-water swimming, you know the clear difference in taste between a salty sea or ocean and a freshwater lake. You don't have to actually drink the water you swim in to know what it tastes like, and let me be very clear, DO NOT drink the water that you swim in! Now that we've gotten that out of the way, the sense of nostalgia associated with these different tastes can have a large impact on how we interpret the environment we're in.

By using all our senses, we can not only gain a greater appreciation for the water but also become more mentally and physically engaged with a workout. The more in tune we become with our environment and senses, the faster we can create mind maps that will improve our performance in the water.

Now that we understand how all our senses can work together, let's discuss the physics of swimming so we can swim faster and smarter than ever before!

"When you change the way you look at things, the things you look at change" - Max Planck, the father of quantum physics

CHAPTER TWO

The Physics of Swimming

THIS CHAPTER IS GOING to blow your mind!

That's a bold statement! Please allow me to explain why I'm so confident that what I'm about to share with you will have a massive impact on your ability to swim more efficiently. I'm going to share exactly how you swim faster. No tricks, gimmicks, or games.

Everything I will share is relatively simple to grasp, backed by science, and can be applied to literally every level of swimmer! Is this too good to be true? Is this Insanity?

"Insanity is doing the same thing over and over again and expecting different results" - Albert Einstein

So, it's technically not insanity, but it would be considered insanity to continue doing the same thing you're currently doing and expect different results! The remarkable thing is that this methodology is not that complicated.

If we break it down, there are only two ways to actually swim faster:

1. Decrease drag.
2. Increase propulsion.

That's it! It's as simple as that. There's no other way to swim faster. Okay, so that's it?? I don't need to finish the book?!

No. It's simple, but it's not THAT simple! In this chapter, I'll get into the science behind how the human body actually moves through the water. We'll talk about fluid dynamics at a super high level and why it matters. Finally, I'll share HOW you actually swim faster using the swimming equation.

The Laws of Physics

Physics dominates the world around us! We usually don't go about our day thinking how gravity, momentum, and acceleration impact our lives. On the flip side, we intuitively ignore some of life's most fascinating phenomena. For example, the Earth is rotating 460 meters per second, roughly 1,000 miles per hour. If that's the case, then why aren't we flying off the face of the planet?

Consider this, air has a density of about 1.2 grams/liter, and water has a density of about 1kg /liter. Air is therefore about 830 times less dense than water. When we swim, it doesn't actually feel 830 times more difficult than walking....well, sometimes it does :)

Swimmers that have a deep understanding of swimming science will be able to master their efficiency and hone their craft. Understanding the science of swimming will help you be more efficient and learn how to better use your time and energy in the water.

How To Float

Science can explain just about every aspect of swimming. Why do some swimmers float and others sink like a rock?

Swimming relies on the nearly-neutral buoyancy of the human body. On average, the body has a relative density of 0.98 compared to water, which causes the average person to feel weightless in the water.

When you're in the water, you float because the water pressure pushes upward and balances your weight. We all have different buoyancies that are determined by our body composition based on how fat and muscle is distributed across our body.

In order to float in water, a person must be less dense than the water. Everyone can float! Some swimmers have a much more difficult time mastering this skill than others due to differences in body composition, but I can assure you that everyone can float!

It doesn't matter how "strong" you are or how "lean" your frame is, you can do it! Recall back to finding your zen; that's why this is really important.

You must first be calm, relaxed, and willing to "let go" in the water. If you tense up, it simply will not work, and you'll sink like a rock. If you're a more advanced swimmer, floating efficiency is still crucial because it allows you to tap into your fine motor skills that allow you to swim with less effort and gracefully float above the water as you swim!

. . .

Drag

As I mentioned at the start of the chapter, there are only two fundamental ways to swim faster: by decreasing drag or increasing propulsion. Let's first discuss decreasing drag because this will allow you to improve the most in the shortest amount of time.

At some point in our lives, we've stuck our hand out the window of a moving car and noticed the changes in air resistance based on how our hand was positioned. If we keep our hand parallel to the ground, we'll feel less wind resistance than if we hold it perpendicular with our fingertips pointing to the sky.

This same concept applies in the water as well. In fluid dynamics, drag (sometimes called resistance) is the force acting opposite to the relative motion of the object (our body) with respect to a surrounding fluid (water). Without getting too much into the weeds (or bubbles), just know that the movement of the water around your body while you're swimming is referred to as "flow".

There are four elements that interrupt this flow and cause frontal drag: your body position, surface area, swim gear, and speed. The faster you swim, the stronger the frontal drag becomes. This makes swimming with proper technique even more crucial the faster you swim.

How To Decrease Drag

The most dramatic way you can decrease drag is by improving your body position. This simply means the way your body floats (or sinks) in the water. A good body position allows you to swim "high" in the water with minimal points of resistance along your body-line.

Imagine for a second that your body is a Hydroplane! This nimble watercraft is able to plane over the water at over 300 kilometers per hour. Now imagine that same motorboat pulling an anchor 5 meters below the surface of the water.

Surely the drag of the anchor in addition to the lower overall position of the watercraft would make the hydroplane move at a fraction of the speed. Our bodies function the same way in the water. In this analogy, your legs are the anchor, and your body position is the hull of the hydroplane.

The single biggest component of drag on the human body after our head and chest is our legs. Similar to a hydroplane dragging the anchor, our legs can cause our entire body to sink in the water. If an elite swimmer raises his or her hip position in the water by just one centimeter, that could be the difference between making an Olympic team and breaking a world record.

For a beginner swimmer, in just one 30 minute session, you might be able to raise your hip position by half a meter and swim 5 seconds faster per 25 meters. Over one kilometer, that's nearly four minutes faster.

This type of almost-immediate reduction in time is absolutely incredible. You will not find any other tool, swimsuit, or strategy that can make you improve more quickly than raising your body position in the water.

So how do you go about improving your body position? The answer is as simple as the question: Just look at the bottom of the pool when you swim.

Is it really that easy? Yes, it is! Your head position leads your overall body posture in the water. If you look up, your hips will sink like a rock. If you look down at the bottom and maintain a neutral head position, your body will float behind your head.

This is no different than having a good standing posture. Try this fun exercise. Close this book and place it on top of your head. Keep your eyes level and look at something directly in front of you. Once you've found your balance, picture yourself laying on your stomach with the same posture. This is the proper body position in swimming.

It's the fundamental position that all competitive stroke technique is based off of. This is because, when you're in the proper streamline body position, your body has the least amount of drag on it. Your body occupies the least surface area and displaces the least amount of water.

Think about this fundamental body position for every stroke you swim and every time you push off the wall. Many swimmers prematurely lift the head up to breath or simply look for the wall.

I promise you, the wall is not moving, just keep your eyes down on the bottom. Most pools have a black line on the bottom in designated lap lanes. It's there for your benefit to swim in a straight line without having to worry about where you're going.

Most pools also have a T on the bottom near the wall on each side of the pool to signify when the black line is ending and the wall is nearing. It's important to familiarize yourself with every pool you swim and use these features to your advantage. If you're swimming in open water, this is even easier. Just look down, you probably won't be able to see the bottom anyway.

We've discussed how to decrease drag so that you can reduce resistance in the water. This foundation in physics and a proper understanding of body positioning will serve as the basis for all future stroke discussion in this book and online material.

Increasing Propulsion

When I imagine the word propulsion, I think of a rocket-ship taking off! A typical rocket produces more than a million pounds of thrust that allows it to carry more than 6,000 pounds at speeds topping 22,000 miles per hour!

So how do we swim like a rocket-ship without burning tons of rocket fuel?

Luckily for us, our bodies are much more efficient than rockets because we can "re-launch" every time we push off the wall. Additionally, we can actually increase our propulsion without changing our physical shape or strength in the water.

Propulsion is improved first and foremost by working on stroke mechanics and then becoming efficient in applying that technique in the water. The combined effects of body balance, streamlining, and good stroke mechanics are what yield faster swimming.

Early Vertical Forearm (EVF)

I want you to think of your hand as a giant paddle in the water! If you want to pull more water, you need a bigger paddle, right?

Well, sort of, not really! You see, even though you can't make your hand bigger, you can actually increase the surface area of your "paddle" by improving your technique and timing of the pull.

This sounds crazy right? It's a concept called EVF.

EVF is short for "Early Vertical Forearm." It's one of the most commonly referenced concepts in the technical swimming and coaching world, yet most swimmers are unsure what it is and how to use it to swim faster.

The idea is you use your entire arm to pull water rather than just your hand. Let's break this down!

By focusing on pulling water with your forearm, you can increase the surface area of your "paddle" and therefore swim faster.

The goal is to position your forearm as close to vertical as possible in the catch phase of the stroke to grab the most water as early as possible. Rather than pulling straight down, it's important to initiate the catch with the fingertips.

By doing this, you will increase the surface area of your pull. Your forearm/arm has much more surface area than just your hand. We'll discuss how this applies to each stroke in future chapters.

Increasing Propulsion Drill

A great drill to develop this skill in all four strokes is called "fist drill." This is where you ball up your hand into a fist, and swim in 25m or 50m increments focusing on initiating an early vertical forearm. After a few hundred meters swimming like this, when you open your hands and swim "normally," your hands will feel HUGE!

You'll feel as though the surface area of your hands just increased by 10-20%. It feels incredible, and this drill can be applied to all the competitive strokes.

. . .

Open Finger Swimming

Is it better to keep your hands cupped and fingers together when you swim or to let your fingers spread apart?

Let's try an experiment together. Take one of your hands and press all your fingers together as tight as you can. After you've made a watertight seal between your fingers, press your hand on the table in front of you. Press down into the table with your palm and fingertips and feel how much control and power you have.

Now, lift your hand off the table and open your fingers as wide as they go like you're a server in a restaurant carrying a massive tray of food. Now repeat the process of pressing down on the table and feel how much power you have. Press your hand into the table and feel the level of control and balance you have from your thumb all the way to your pinkie finger.

When it comes to swimming, this experiment can be applied in the water as well. Believe it or not, you actually pull more water with your fingers slightly separated. Now I'm not saying you should swim with your fingers spread apart, like Spiderman crawling up a wall.

In fact, that would be much slower than swimming with your hands squeezed together. The perfect spread between fingers varies from person to person, but as a general guide, your fingertips should be 5-10mm apart.

So, why is it faster to swim with your fingers slightly apart?

It comes down to physics! As your hand moves through the water, the layer of water around your hands and between your fingers moves as well. This "sticky" layer of water surrounding your fingers increases the surface area of your hand. The force of the water will slightly flatten the skin on the fingers, creating a webbed effect, similar to a duck or a frog.

Numerous studies have proven this to be true. A 2012 study published in the Journal of Theoretical Biology found that a hand with fingers spread slightly exerts a 5-10% greater force than a hand with fingers held tightly together. This study also found that when compared to fingers spread wide, a slight spread between fingers produced a 5-10% greater force!

In fact, researchers at the American Physical Society Division of Fluid Dynamics concluded that a finger spread of just 10° (5-10mm) could boost a swimmer's speed by 2.5% compared to swimming with fingers held together.

For example, if you swim a 25-second 50-meter freestyle, you could drop a full ½ second by implementing this finger spread technique. That's insane!

The Swimming Equation

Swimming can be a really technical sport, but it doesn't have to be that difficult. If you can break it down into its fundamental components, you can gain a new appreciation for the sport and swim faster and smarter than ever before.

If you want to get technical, I present to you the "swimming equation"

$$ST = (UT + TT) + (CC*SR)$$

This equation is designed to help demonstrate how manipulating certain attributes of the stroke impacts your overall swimming time. Like all equations, it's made up of different variables. In later chapters, we'll dive into how you can actually manipulate these variables to swim faster.

$$ST = (UT + TT) + (CC*SR)$$

$$ST = (UT + TT) + (CC*SR)$$
ST = Swimming Time
UT = Underwater Time
TT = Turn Time
CC = Cycle Count
SR = Stroke Rate

The swimming equation represents two components: underwater time and overwater time. Underwater time is made up of the time spent underwater plus the time you spend turning at the wall. The overwater time is a function of Cycle Count multiplied by Stroke Rate. The units for Stroke Rate is in seconds/stroke.

So, how do you swim faster?

1. Decrease Cycle Count. In other words, take fewer strokes and maximize distance per stroke. The key is maintain stroke rate while doing this.
2. Increase Stroke Rate. This means to swim at a faster tempo. Again, you must maintain distance per stroke.

3. Do Both: Decrease Cycle Count and increase Stroke
    Rate.

In order of difficulty, decreasing Cycle Count is by far the
easiest and will deliver the highest return on time invested in
the water. By focusing on improving your efficiency, you're
decreasing resistance in the water and therefore maximizing
distance per stroke. It's much harder to increase tempo while
maintaining Cycle Count because this requires increasing
propulsion. Increasing propulsion is much harder as it will only
come through seasonal training.

To apply this to training, focus on maximizing distance per
stroke. The easiest component to improve is distance per
stroke. I advise working on tempo separate from distance per
stroke.

This gives you a chance to focus on one particular component of the swimming equation without compromise to the
other parts. Focus on maintaining tempo while increasing
distance per stroke. Finally, do sets that focus on SWOLF!

SWOLF

SWOLF is basically a measure of how efficient you are in
your swimming. SWOLF is swimming's equivalent of Par
(score). It's calculated by taking the number of strokes you take
in one length of swimming added to your time (in seconds)
over that distance. This score is then normalized to a 25m pool
distance.

Similar to Golf, you should focus on reducing your total

score. A really simple example is swimming 25m in 25 seconds with 20 arm strokes. Your SWOLF is 45! Remember, similar to Golf, your goal is to decrease this number so that you can become as efficient as possible.

If you can swim the same 25m distance in 23 seconds while maintaining 20 arm strokes, your SWOLF score just dropped to 43! It's really important to only benchmark your SWOLF score against yourself. Focus on improving this over a period of time, and you'll be well on your way!

Swimming can be complicated, but it doesn't have to be! If you break it up into these fundamental components and focus on the only two elements that make you swim faster—decreasing drag and increasing propulsion—it will be much simpler to not only understand how to improve, but it will also be more fun as well. You'll find ways to improve your swimming that you never thought were possible!

CHAPTER THREE

How to Write a Swim Workout

MANY SWIMMERS JUMP in the pool and swim back and forth with no plan. Maybe the goal is to swim continuously for 30 minutes, hit 10 laps, or swim 1,000 meters. Whatever your approach is, there's no wrong way to go about it, and if your plan works for you, that's awesome!

If you're looking to take your swimming to the next level, then adding a bit of structure will help you improve your swimming like never before! Someone who used to swim continuously and then switches to following structured workouts in a plan will see an almost immediate improvement in technique, speed, and confidence in the water.

I've seen this scenario play out time and time again for countless members of the MySwimPro global community. Not everyone can afford a personal coach to provide specific workouts designed to meet certain goals and time demands. This is why I created MySwimPro, a personal coach in your pocket, and it's why I wrote this book!

What is your swimming goal?

Understanding how a workout is structured will allow you to maximize your time in the water. Before you write any swim workout for yourself or follow a plan, the first step is figuring out the goal you're trying to achieve!

Are you trying to lose weight? Improve endurance? Enhance speed? Refine technique?

If you're like many swimmers, you might have some or all of those goals listed above. More advanced swimmers can focus on specific skills like breath control, flip turns, pace, or underwater dolphin kick.

Having a clear idea of your goal before getting started will not only give you more focus when you swim but will pave the way for a better guided workout experience.

Once you know the goal of the workout, you next determine the optimal outcome of the training session or plan. In other words, what measurable output are you trying to achieve by the end of the workout or plan?

Maybe you want to achieve a certain time in a race. Perhaps you're looking to swim a specific distance confidently without stopping. Whatever the outcome of your goal is, write it down! We'll come back to the concept of SMART goal setting at the end of the book!

Workout Structure

There are five main parts to a swim workout. Not all of them need to be used in every workout. Typically a swim workout will have a "Warmup," "Main Set," and "Cool Down." Sometimes there's an additional grouping before or after the "Main Set" called a "Pre Set" or "Post Set."

- Warm Up: 10-20% of the workout. Activate your body and prepare your muscles for the main set. Gradually build up your heart rate.
- Main Set: 60-80% of the workout. This is the main focus of your workout.
- Cool Down: 10-20% of the workout. Lower your heart rate and flush out lactic acid from your muscles.

Understanding the structure of the workout will allow you to have the most efficient and powerful workouts. To start, let's look at a set. An individual set is a specific way that you'll do a certain number of repetitions, over a certain distance, with a certain stroke type in a specified amount of rest.

Interval Training

Interval training is a really important concept to understand because it will allow you to get the most efficient aerobic training. The total interval is a factor of your total swim time plus total rest time. You can have an interval based on the number of breaths taken or simply rest time.

The most standard form of interval training in competitive swimming is swim time + rest time.

Example Set: 4 x 100s Freestyle @ 2:00

- Repetitions: 4
- Distance: 100 meters
- Stroke Type: Freestyle
- Interval: 2:00 (including both swim time and rest time)

What this means is, if you can swim a 100 freestyle in 90 seconds, you'll have 30 seconds rest before leaving for the next repetition. 4 x 100s Freestyle @ 2:00 will take 8:00. If it takes you 90 seconds to swim each 100, then your total set time will be 8:00, even though you only swam for 6:00.

Benefits of Interval Training

Whether you're a novice exerciser or you've been working out for years, interval training can help you jazz up your workout routine. Before going deeper into workout structure, I want to reflect on some of the massive benefits of interval training:

1. You'll Improve Technique: By taking repetitive but short breaks, you will train your body to only swim at a higher body position and at greater speed.
2. You'll Burn More Calories: Taking short breaks in the workout allows you to train at a higher intensity and thus elevate your heart rate (which helps you get the health benefits of a cardio routine, including weight loss, if that's your goal).
3. Improved Aerobic Capacity: As your cardiovascular fitness improves, you'll be able to train longer, faster, and more efficiently.
4. Added Variety: Swimming the same routine over and over can get monotonous. When you do interval training, there is no limit to what you can accomplish.
5. No Equipment Needed: All you need is a pace clock at the pool or on your wrist. Even if you don't have a

clock, you can do interval training by breath count between repetitions. An easy way to do this is to count how many breaths you take once you touch the wall, and then push off for the next length after taking a predetermined number of breaths.

After factoring in all these benefits, I hope you've at least considered giving interval training a go at your next workout. Your future self will thank you!

Complex Set Structure

Sometimes there will be multiple sets together inside one part of the workout. These sets that are grouped together are collectively called "Set-Groups." These groups of sets will sometimes have a bracket around them instructing that each set-group be completed multiple times.

For example, instead of doing the main set once-through, you could do the entire main set group for two, three, or four rounds. This is most common for the Main Set group and sometimes for the set immediately before or after the Main Set group. Here's an example below:

Warmup
   1 x 200 Freestyle @ 4:00
   4 x 50 Kick @ 1:20

Drill Set

4 x 25 Drill @ :40

4 x 25 Drill @ :40

Main Set (2x)

    4 x 100 Freestyle @ 2:00

    4 x 75 Freestyle @ 1:30

    4 x 50 Freestyle @ 1:00

    4 x 25 Freestyle @ :30

Cool Down

    4 x 50 Freestyle @ 1:00

In this workout example, doubling the Main Set would add another 1,000 meters to the workout. As you can see, there's a lot of manipulation that can be done to the actual workout structure that leaves the fundamental components in place but can drastically change the overall impact of the workout.

When you do a drill set before the main set, the goal is to apply whatever skill you were working on in the drill set into the main set.

Workout Density

It's also important to be mindful of workout density, or, the amount of swimming you're doing per unit of time. If you're swimming a 1,000-meter workout in 30 minutes, that is considered less "dense" than doing the same 1,000-meter workout in only 20 minutes.

Rest time plays a big role in workout density. If you don't give yourself enough rest during your warm up, you may not be able to perform well during the main set, which should be the focus of your workout! I always advise that you want to feel your best by the end of the workout.

You want to leave the pool feeling great so the next time you swim, you can pick up where you left off! Oftentimes, swimmers get this backwards. Countless times at the pool, I have seen swimmers spin their wheels in the first 2-3 minutes and become burned out after just 10 minutes. Save some gas in the tank to finish strong. You'll get more out of the workout and leave the pool feeling more satisfied.

Training Zones

Training zones help organize a swim workout into different intensities by assigning a specific "zone" to each set. Although this is a more advanced attribute to workouts, there is a big benefit to understanding it!

A foundation in training zones will help maximize your understanding of structured workouts in the MySwimPro app or any other swim workout you might see online or on a whiteboard at the pool.

To keep things simple, we'll overview the seven training zones:

- Recovery (Rec)
- Endurance 1 (EN1)
- Endurance 2 (EN2)
- Endurance 3 (EN3)
- Sprint 1 (SP1)

- Sprint 2 (SP2)
- Sprint 3 (SP3)

The first four zones represent "endurance" zones, and the last three zones represent "anaerobic" zones. Coach Jon Urbanchek of the University of Michigan suggested color-coding each energy category for ease of understanding.

These zones are color coded and explained in detail in the MySwimPro app. There's no one-size fits all approach for color coding, so it's common to see workouts on whiteboards on pool decks with what seem to be bizarre colors labeled next to sets.

In the MySwimPro app, we further simplified the zones by labeling them with a more friendly title that describes the intensity. Here they are below:

ZONE	TITLE	DESCRIPTION
RECOVERY	EASY	Cool down & recovery sets. Typically done after race pace and sprint sets.
EN1	MODERATE	Warm up & drill sets. Pace that could be swum for long durations where maintaining stroke technique requires concentration.
EN2	ENDURANCE	Cruise pace; can be held for extended periods of time. Breathing and stroke are rhythmed and become strained after ~ 10 minutes.
EN3	THRESHOLD	Short rest; edge of aerobic threshold. Pace that is primarily taxing your VO2 Max system. Can be maintained for only 5-10 minutes.
SP1	BEST AVERAGE	Extremely hard efforts that can be maintained for the duration of the total set's distance.
SP2	RACE PACE	The maximum pace that can be held for a single repetition of a set; lactate.
SP3	SPRINT	Focus on speed, power, and tempo; taxes the neuromuscular system. Cannot be maintained for more than 60 seconds.

The importance of training zones in swimming is based on the existence of several different pathways to recycle energy in the muscle cells during exercise. The main pathways of energy recycling are non-aerobic metabolism (creatine phosphate), anaerobic metabolism (anaerobic glycolysis), and aerobic metabolism.

Metabolism is the process of storing and releasing the energy. Energy for the body is stored in different forms, and pathways are used to convert these forms into accessible energy that an athlete can use to perform work. There are no "borders" to energy pathways in a body.

At any given time, several pathways, not just one, may be engaged in energy production, but dominance of an energy source depends on the duration and intensity of the exercise. Usually workload is broken into several energy "zones" based on the duration and intensity of the training.

ZONE	TITLE	Set Distance (m)	Set Duration (min)	HR (% of max)	Work : Rest	Sample Set (Advanced Swimmer)
RECOVERY	EASY			< 70	N/A	
EN1	MODERATE			70 - 80		
EN2	ENDURANCE			80 - 90		
SP1						
SP2	RACE PACE					
SP3	SPRINT					

Energy "zones" allow you to develop a specific pathway of energy recycling and to quantify, track, and plan the physiological adaptations desired for the specific set.

Different swimming events require the training of different energy pathways. The same swimming set can be swum in different energy zones. For example, you can swim sets with higher or lower intensities. This will recruit different pathways of energy recycling.

The same swimming intensity, or even heart rate, affects the energy recycling pathways differently when you're at different stages of the season (i.e., in the beginning of the season, after a sickness, or at peak performances).

Luckily, with the MySwimPro app, you don't have to worry about writing workouts, designing set structure, choosing intervals, or planning out zones. We take care of all that for you.

Hurray for software!

Seasonal Planning

The success of a season starts with planning! Whether you're a coach or athlete, it's important to plan the season with the desired end results in mind. It can be difficult to think long-term, but as the quote goes:

If you fail to plan, you are planning to fail - Benjamin Franklin

Building a successful yearly training plan starts with periodizing training around major competitions or specific goals. Once you've mastered this process, you'll be that much closer to achieving your goals!

This final section of the chapter will be most relevant to swim coaches and swimmers designing highly specific and personalized plans for themselves. If you prefer to follow a structured plan in the MySwimPro App, jump to the next chapter. If you're a swimmer and want to nerd out about seasonal periodization, let's dive in!

What is Periodization?

Periodizing an exercise program aims to optimize training during short (weeks, or months) as well as long periods of time (years, or an athletic career) to produce maximum gains in physical performance. The goal of periodization is to be able to achieve peak performance at a particular time, such as at a major competition at the end of the season.

1 YEAR
MACROCYCLE
MESOCYCLES
MICROCYCLES
INDIVIDUAL SESSIONS

Structuring the Season

Macrocycles are seasonal or year-long plans. First, determine the date of the key competition where a peak performance is desired. The season could be a year in length, six months in length, or, as with some high school seasons, only 10 weeks in length.

Mesocycles are training periods of approximately six to eight weeks. An effective training period allows a swimmer to benefit from adaptations of the body that are a result of training. As a general rule of thumb, the body will need roughly six weeks to make significant physical and chemical changes in its ability to provide energy to the muscles.

Microcycles are generally weeklong training periods, but they can range from 4-10 days in length. Determine what the training emphasis will be in each training block. This does not mean that ONLY one specific type of work will be done; however, this will be the training emphasis during that training block. Plan each week's emphasis, then plan what will be emphasized each day, each practice. Don't forget to plan rest and recovery into the schedule.

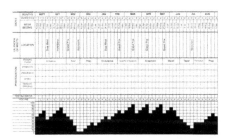

Keep in mind that there are no real boundaries or borders between blocks or cycles. All changes of training emphasis should be gradual.

The four Meso Cycles below are typical of one Macro Cycle!

1. General Preparation
2. Specific Preparation
3. Competition Phase
4. Transition Phase

The Science Behind Periodization

The goal is to create chemical changes at the cellular level and foster physiological adaptation. This takes weeks (often months). John Leonard of the American Swim Coaches Association stresses three key variables when it comes to building workouts that include varying...

- Intensity – how much effort is being applied in sets (energy zones)
- Load Density – how much swimming is done in a period of time (EX: 1,000meters/15minutes of training)
- Load Volume – total amount of work done in a measured time frame (total distance)

Execute and Evaluate

After each season, it's important to evaluate! What were your goals? Did you meet them? How did technique, training, and performance evolve over each of the cycles and across the entire season?

This is your chance to analyze what happened and where improvements could be made so your time is spent most efficiently achieving your goals!

Remember, the definition of insanity is doing the same thing over and over again, but expecting different results. Learn from what worked, adapt, and keep it moving!

MAIN SET

Swimming Technique

CHAPTER FOUR

Technique 101

I TRULY BELIEVE that everyone is just one day away from achieving their Gold Medal Moment.

You don't have to win gold to achieve something great! I know that with the right guidance, structure, and support, you can make your goals a reality.

One of the first steps in that swimming journey is refining your stroke technique. We all approach swimming with different skills, flexibility, and strengths. Despite the diversity of our background, there are core underlying principles for each of the competitive strokes.

In this section of the book, I encourage you to reference the complementary video library available in the online course to see the swimming technique and drills mentioned. Adding a visual element helps illustrate these foundational principles in each stroke.

Additionally, I strongly encourage you to learn about all of the strokes covered in this section. I often get asked the question, "why should I swim anything other than freestyle?!" I think I could write an entire book on that topic alone! I'll spare you the details and share the TL;DR version: swimming every stroke improves your feel of the water, engages more muscles (and thus, burns more calories), and adds variety to the workout for mental stimulation.

What is Perfect Technique?

A couple of years after launching MySwimPro, I created a video titled, "How To Swim Freestyle With Perfect Technique." In this video I stood in front of a whiteboard and shared six foundational principles of the freestyle stroke. What seemed like a basic video at the time has now been viewed millions of times.

The response to that video has been incredible, and I'm thrilled to include it along with many more in the online course content. The comments viewers left in the comment section of this video are incredible and one of the reasons I created more content like that and even wrote this book.

The idea of "perfect technique" is something worth discussing before diving into each stroke individually. "Perfection" is a goal that will forever remain impossible for any human being to achieve. By definition, perfection is the action or process of improving something until it is faultless.

In swimming (and in life) there is no such thing as "perfection". Understanding this, the only achievable goal is to strive to become the best that you can possibly be. No swimmer has "perfect technique". We are always pushing ourselves to be better, and that is what I encourage you to do when you think about applying these techniques to your own swimming and in life!

Swimming History

Freestyle is the fastest and most efficient stroke in the water. But before we dive into the mechanics, I'd like to take a step back and share a little bit of swimming history with you!

The "front crawl" style of swimming has been in use since ancient times. Archeologists have discovered bas relief sculptures in Egypt that illustrate swimming dating back to 2000 BCE. It wasn't until 1896 that swimming made its first appearance in the modern Olympics in Athens, Greece.

The men's 100 meter freestyle was one of the four swimming events that took place in Athens. There were just 13 total participants and no Olympic 50-meter pool. Instead, all swimming events were held off of the Piraeus coast at the Bay of Zea where the water temperature ranged from 11-13° Celsius (53-57° Fahrenheit).

Can you imagine what that must have been like??

"Freestyle" is not actually a stroke but a category in swimming competition. The most common and popular stroke in freestyle races is the front crawl because this type of swimming is the fastest. For example in a 50 meter freestyle race, swimmers can theoretically swim butterfly, backstroke, breaststroke, or front crawl during the race.

I've actually done this several times myself. The look on the timer's face behind my lane after the race was precious. As fun as this sounds, I do not advise swimming anything other than front crawl in a freestyle race unless you have a very specific reason for doing so, such as recording an official qualifying time for a future competition.

I know this sounds like a lot of semantics, but to keep things simple, the term "freestyle" will be used as a synonym for "front crawl," and in this book and in most swimming contexts, when referring to "freestyle" it will most likely mean "front crawl".

Short Axis vs. Long Axis

There are a few reasons why Freestyle is the most efficient way to move through the water and also the fastest style of swimming. One of those reasons has to do with how your body is positioned in the water during all phases of the stroke.

If you recall, there are only two ways to swim faster: reduce drag or increase propulsion. In Freestyle and Backstroke, your body is positioned flat at the surface of the water and therefore displaces the least amount of water and thus the least resistance.

To take this concept a step further, when you swim freestyle and backstroke, your body rotates horizontally side to side along a center axis point. This center axis starts in the middle of the top of your head and extends down through your spine.

Both freestyle and backstroke are considered long-axis strokes for this reason. This is a really important concept to understand because the way you swim these two strokes and also train them is very different from butterfly and breaststroke.

Butterfly and breaststroke are considered "short-axis" strokes. Rather than rotation around a center axis that extends from the head through the spine, in butterfly and backstroke, you pivot the upper part of your body using your hips as a horizontal axis point.

This fundamental difference between short axis and long axis strokes changes how you should train these strokes. For example, due to the increase in resistance that both breaststroke and butterfly pose as short axis strokes, you can't endure as much distance without sacrificing quality stroke technique.

From a competition perspective, both breaststroke and butterfly should be primarily swum at race pace or close to race pace as often as possible. This also means shorter repetition distances and also more rest. It is really difficult swimming butterfly for an extended period of time. It's also near impossible to swim "slow butterfly" while maintaining good technique.

On the flip side, it's relatively simple to swim freestyle at any number of speeds (particularly slower) for extended durations without faltering the stroke mechanics. Therefore, we often find ourselves swimming freestyle as the primary stroke to increase aerobic capacity and also as a way to develop a feel of the water for beginners.

Streamline

Streamline is the fundamental body position in swimming. All four competitive strokes are built off of a streamline body line. If you recall back to the discussion on physics, reducing drag is the most impactful way to swim faster.

Streamline is used when you push off the wall or dive in the water. Your goal is to make your body as narrow as possible displacing the least amount of water. You want to imagine yourself as a torpedo pushing off the wall. This means your body is in alignment from fingertips to toes and your overall body position is parallel to the surface of the water and bottom of the pool.

This is a skill that everyone can improve in!

It doesn't matter if you're just getting started or an olympic swimmer. EVERYONE can improve their streamline body position when they push off the wall or dive in. The reason this is so important is not only because it sets up your body posture for all of the strokes, but also because you will never swim faster than when you push off the wall in streamline.

The better your streamline off the wall, the more speed you will carry into your first few strokes. This bonus speed you get from pushing off the wall is something that should be leveraged even if your primary goal is open water swimming and triathlon. Despite not being able to push off the wall in the open sea, teaching your body how to swim "fast" in those first few strokes sets up your speed for the rest of that length of the pool.

The biggest mistake swimmers make with their streamline is not having their head in a neutral position. Basically looking forward at your hands when you push off the wall. This is relatively easy to improve. Just look down at the bottom of the pool and stretch your fingers forward as far as you can. Let's try a dryland drill together.

Dryland Drill for Head Positioning

Put down this book. Stand up. With your feet pressed together, stand tall, and lock your eyes on something immediately at your eye level. Next, place one hand over the other lining up your fingers and use the thumb on the top hand to wrap around and grab the hand underneath.

Now the second to last step is to raise your arms above your head keeping your hands in the same position. If you're flexible enough, straighten out your arms so your elbows are locked out. Squeeze your arms together focusing on getting your elbows closer to each other.

At this point, you feel pretty narrow and have mastered the streamline, but there's still one more step! Stand on your tippy toes and stretch your fingers up so the top of your middle finger is now 10 centimeters higher than when you started.

If you're in a public place and people are looking at you, this is amazing! You can relax now :)

This is a fantastic drill that you can do periodically through the day to stretch your body, improve your flexibility and also increase circulation. This principle of elongating your frame is nothing new. There's a scientific reason torpedoes are engineered to be long and narrow.

Your body is a torpedo ready to blast off. The more you focus on applying this principle of elongating your body and holding your streamline tight when you push off the wall, the more speed you'll transfer into your strokes on top of the water.

A great drill to amplify this concept in the water is simply pushing off the wall as hard as you can in order to streamline and then floating until you stop. Try this the next time you go to the pool. How far can you float just by pushing off the wall in streamline. No kicking at all.

Did you go 5 meters? 10 meters? 15 meters?

The more times you practice this, the better you'll get. It's exciting to see your progress after just a few attempts. This same drill can be done diving into the water. The best swimmers in the world can float a full 25 meters off a dive. As incredible as that sounds, these athletes didn't start that way. It takes a consistent focus over the course of years (sometimes decades) to improve streamline to the point of achieving those results.

CHAPTER FIVE

Freestyle

FREESTYLE (or front crawl) is the most efficient and fastest style of swimming. In fact, it is the chosen stroke for all marathon swimmers because of how far you can go without stopping. Here's the proof:

The longest distance ever swum without flippers in the open sea is 225 kilometers (139.8 miles)! I know that sounds insane, doesn't it? This swim in Italy was across the Adriatic Sea from Grado to Riccione. It took Veljko Rogošić of Croatia 50 hours and 10 minutes to complete! It was swum 100% using the freestyle stroke!

Not only is freestyle a stroke you can swim continuously but also into older age. When Veljko Rogošić swam the 225 kilometer trek across the Adriatic Sea, he was 65 years young. So, not only is freestyle the most efficient, but there is also hope for swimmers of any age!

. . .

Head Position

To start, we're going to break down the mechanics of the freestyle stroke into a few core elements! The first being the brains behind the operation—our head!

If we make the analogy of our body relative to a torpedo, our head is the tip of the rocket. Our head experiences the most resistance with the water and slows us down the most when trying to make forward motion.

Not only does your head cause the most resistance, it also sets the direction for the rest of your body to follow. If the positioning of your head changes by just a few degrees, your body position could sink up to half a meter under the surface of the water.

Recall the chapter on physics where we discussed how air is about 830 times less dense than water. The resistance from your body is the single biggest limiting factor in swimming faster. The primary way you improve this is by adjusting your head's position.

So what does the perfect head position look like?

As I explained with "perfect technique," no swimmer has it. We are always pushing ourselves to be better, and that is what I encourage you to do when you think about applying these techniques to your swimming! Although there may be no perfect technique, there are certainly guidelines to follow.

The first is thinking about keeping your head in a neutral position. What does that mean?

Take this book, or any hardcover textbook, and place it on your head. Standing tall, your eyes should be looking straight in front of you. In this neutral position, your head is in alignment with your spine; you're standing tall, and if you tilt your head to look at your toes or raise your head to look at the ceiling, the book will fall down.

This is how you should think about your head position in the water when you swim. It sounds simple because it really is that easy. When you're on your stomach swimming freestyle, just look down at the bottom of the pool. You should see the black or blue line at the bottom. Use it as your guide to swim in a straight line.

If you're in open water, this can be even easier because either the water is too murky to see anything, or you'll be able to see schools of fish within several meters reach. In both of these environments it's critical to keep your head neutral. This can not be stressed enough.

The water-line should be roughly in the middle of your scalp, meaning at least half of your head is submerged under the surface of the water. I'd go as far to say 70-80% of your head should be underwater and just the top part (20-30%) of your swim cap should be visible.

So what happens if your head is not in this position? You swim more slowly. There's no other way to slice it. But why?

Body Position

Everyone's body has a different equilibrium point of buoyancy when in the water. Regardless of your buoyancy, one thing is certain, if any point of your body (head, arms, legs) rises above the surface of the water, the opposite end of your body will sink to balance and return to a new equilibrium position.

Think of your body as a seesaw. If you raise your head, your legs will sink. If you raise your legs (if you can), your head will submerge. Your body is like a scale of checks and balances. The major difference between your body and a seesaw is that your body is not equally distributed in buoyancy.

Your upper body is significantly more buoyant than your lower body and as a result this seesaw analogy is amplified if you raise your head. It's relatively easy for your upper body to stay buoyant and float. Your legs on the other hand depend on downward pressure from your head to keep your body level. A great drill to focus on proper head position is swimming with a paddle on your forehead.

Paddle Drill

Grab a flat hand paddle and remove the straps. Place it on your head just as you placed the book on your head to find a neutral head position. As you swim, the water pressure caused by the resistance of the paddle will keep the paddle pressed against your head. The faster you go, the easier this becomes because there is more pressure being applied to keep the paddle on your head.

If you move your head position even a little, the paddle will not stick. This neutral head position with the paddle applies to when you breathe as well. You should be able to rotate your head to the side while maintaining a neutral head position and keep the paddle pressed against your head. Remember, the goal of this drill is to keep your head in a neutral position so that the rest of your body remains high in the water and therefore reduces overall drag!

A more advanced drill to try is swimming with a cup on the top of your head. This drill will challenge even the most advanced swimmers. Focus on balancing a cup, ideally half full with water, on the top of the head and keep your eyes on the bottom of the pool. Any lateral deviation or up and down movement will cause the cup fall of your head.

The Pull Phase

Now that our head position is as prime and proper as it will ever be, let's focus on what you do with your arms! In this section, we're discussing how to increase propulsion (part two of how to swim more quickly).

As a baseline in freestyle, I want you to always keep your elbows above your hands. Think of this as a rule. Certainly in life, there are those who break the law, but for the scope of this chapter, let's abide by the rules and follow this concept.

Keeping your elbows above your hands applies both above and below the surface of the water. In freestyle, when your hands are above the surface of the water, this is called the recovery phase of the stroke. When your hands are underwater, this is the pull phase.

Your fingertips should enter the water middle finger first about half a meter in front of your shoulders at about a 45° angle to the surface of the water. You want to feel like you're sliding your hands into the water. It should be clean and with minimal splash. Any bubbles at this point in the stroke will simply interrupt with what comes next, so it's important to have a "clean" hand entry into the water led by your middle finger first.

Once your fingertips slide into the water, it's important to extend horizontally just under the surface before anything else. Oftentimes, swimmers will have their hand enter the water and initiate a pull immediately. This is not as efficient as leveraging the forward momentum your body already has and reaching your fingertips further just centimeters below the surface.

Early Vertical Forearm

Once your fingertips have extended and your arm is fully submerged below the surface, then you can start the pull phase. At this point, your body position will have rotated slightly so you're slightly towards your side. If you're flat, this means you have not fully stretched your fingers forward. Next, you'll initiate what's called an EVF, short for Early Vertical Forearm.

If you recall from the prior physics chapter, this is to increase your pulling surface area so that you can pull more water. Rather than just pulling your arms straight down, focus on bending your elbow and positioning your forearm to become vertical. This will increase the plane of pulling force by extending your leverage from your fingertips all the way to your elbow.

The first few hundred arm strokes you focus on this, it will feel weird. After a few thousand strokes with intentional focus, this will start to feel normal. Then, after a few million strokes, you'll have developed a strong feel of the water that leverages the illusive early vertical forearm.

If that sounds intimidating, it doesn't have to be, and I'm going to share with you a drill progression that can speed this process up 10x. That's right, if you follow the progression below, you'll be able to pick this skill up in an order of magnitude less time. Here's how it works.

Drill Progression for EVF

You'll start with fist drill. Ball up your hand in a tight fist and swim one or two lengths of the pool focusing on catching the water with your forearm. This is supposed to feel slow because the surface area of your hand has been reduced significantly. After struggling to swim 50, 100, or 200 meters with tight fists, next, open your pointer finger on both hands.

Swim another few lengths focusing on entering the water with your pointer finger, and only your pointer finger. After a few lengths, add your middle finger so now you're swimming with your hand in a fist with your pointer finger and middle finger sticking out. Be sure to follow the drill progression in this order to avoid offending your fellow swimmers and lifeguards at the pool :)

Next, add your thumb. Swim a few lengths.

Finally, open up your hands and swim "all natural" with the intense focus on catching the water with an early vertical forearm. If you follow this progression just a few times, you'll feel a noticeable difference in how your arms and entire body connect with the water.

Breathing

Many people can swim what seems to be flawless freestyle until they need to take a breath. Unless you were born with gills, you'll be out of luck in the pool if you don't know how to breathe easily when you swim.

Notice how I used the word "easily." Breathing in all four competitive strokes should feel easy, effortless, and repeatable. In order to do this, we need to take a step back and talk about the basics of breathing and blowing bubbles.

When we learned how to swim, the first skill that was taught was blowing bubbles before submerging underwater. We learned a very simple concept. Above the water, we breathe in, and below the water, we breathe out. More specifically, above the water we breathe in through our mouths, and under the water we breathe out through our nose in a controlled humming pattern.

While this sounds basic, it's fundamental to sustained swimming, not just freestyle, but any form of swimming. When we swim freestyle, we need to focus on maintaining a controlled exhale through our nose when our face is under the water. As we rotate to the side to breathe, there should be a mini burst exhalation and just enough time to inhale enough air through our mouth before returning to our neutral head position.

When you rotate to the side to breathe, try to keep one eye under the surface of the water. Remember, about 70% of your head should be submerged while maintaining your neutral head position. Because you're making forward progress, your head will create a natural air pocket when you rotate to breathe. When your arm is fully extended, this is your opportunity to breathe and inhale on your side opposite to the arm that's extended.

Rotation

If you're looking to take your freestyle to the next level, this next section on how rotational momentum can make you swim faster might make all the difference for you.

If you swim with your body flat, you will limit your stroke length by 15-20%. In order to reach maximum distance per stroke every time your arm extends forward, you'll need to rotate your body. This movement depends on using your entire body to drive the rotation. The core focal point of this rotation is your hips.

Your hips drive the rotation and your arms simply follow the motion. This seems somewhat counterintuitive to what actually happens, and that's okay. When you swim, it's easier to think about extending your fingertips forward and then rotating your hips. This works, but it's not as impactful as setting up the rotational drive with your core.

If you can drive rotational power from your diaphragm, you'll create rotational momentum that will then support an increase in your distance per stroke. The degree to which you rotate depends on a few different factors.

In general, the higher your stroke rate, the less you'll rotate to your side on each stroke. In a full effort sprint, you may only rotate 10-15° to each side. When you're swimming more casually, rotation might increase to 30-45° per side. You do not want to fully rotate 90° onto each side because the increase in distance per stroke is negated by a loss of rotational momentum.

Rather than rotate fully to each side, focus on getting half way there with your hips. This is just enough to reach full extension that will increase your distance per stroke while maintaining forward rotational momentum. Although I don't advise full rotation while swimming regular freestyle, this is a great drill to focus on developing balance in the water.

ROTATION DRILL: 3 STROKES + 12 KICKS

A great drill I recommend for swimmers of all levels is called 3 strokes + 12 kicks. This drill can be done with fins for added support. You swim freestyle taking three arm strokes, then on the third stroke rotate to full extension and kick on your side for 12 kicks. After the 12 kicks, take three additional strokes and then balance on your opposite side for another 12 kicks.

This drill focuses on balance and setting up rotational momentum from your core. It's important to remember that this full rotation is not how you swim regular freestyle, it's simply a drill that exaggerates the motion to focus on a specific skill.

If you recall the swimming equation, your overwater time is a result of cycle count multiplied by stroke rate. If you can focus on using rotational momentum to increase your distance per stroke and therefore decrease your cycle count, then you'll swim faster if you're able to maintain your stroke rate.

Kick

Kicking in freestyle is the last technique element I overview, because it is the least impactful to improvement. This is a bold statement! Especially when you consider that our legs are the strongest parts of our body and when we watch the pros swim on TV, it looks like they have a motorboat on their legs propelling them forward.

This is not to say that kicking is not important, quite the opposite, it's extremely important, just not the first place we start when learning the basics. A strong kick can easily make the difference between an Olympian and an average swimmer. Regardless of how strong (or weak) you are at kicking, you can always improve!

Freestyle and Backstroke use the flutter kick. This is where you point your toes, keep your legs straight and move your legs opposite each other in an up and down pattern. The fulcrum for this up and down movement comes from your hips. A big mistake swimmers routinely make is bending knees in the flutter kick. A little bit of knee bend is okay, but the legs should appear almost straight through the entire up and down motion.

The second biggest mistake many swimmers make, and I myself am guilty of this, is having too large of an amplitude (i.e., the total distance your feet travel from the lowest point to the highest point in one kick cycle). This amplitude distance should be less than half a meter. The reason for such a small kick is that any additional propulsion of a bigger kick will be negated by an increase in resistance.

Remember, it's much easier to decrease drag than to increase propulsion, and this concept is amplified through the kick. Think, short and fast. There's no other way to do it in freestyle and backstroke. A great analogy to focus on this is "kicking in a bucket." Imagine fitting both your legs inside a narrow cylindrical tube or bucket.

You must keep your amplitude small enough so that your heels and toes do not hit the bucket when you kick. Think about kicking as fast and short as possible while maintaining this compact technique. This is easiest to practice kicking in streamline on your back. Keep your toes pointed, and knees under the surface of the water.

My final point on kicking technique is simply, don't over-think it! Oftentimes, swimmers, especially beginners, place too much focus on kicking, and it actually takes away from the more important technique elements like head position, the catch, and pull. If anything, I encourage all beginner swimmers to de-emphasize the kick.

Because our legs are the strongest and most muscular parts of our body, they also take up the most energy and blood flow. In a shorter distance sprint, that's not a problem—it should be all cylinders firing at once. Kick as much as your body allows! If you're swimming anything longer than a few minutes, though, you'll want to de-emphasize your legs. You'll be able to swim for a longer period of time, with a better body position and less effort.

CHAPTER SIX

Backstroke

SIMILAR TO FREESTYLE, backstroke is a long axis stroke. Your body rotates upon an axis that leads with your head and runs though your spine. There are many similarities between freestyle and backstroke but also a few key differences. In this chapter, we'll go over all of these stroke specifics in great detail with a holistic focus on technique.

Before we get into the stroke mechanics, it's important to note that backstroke is the best stroke to swim for recovery purposes. We'll get into the details in further chapters when we discuss injury prevention, but to offer a bit of context, swimming backstroke is great for your shoulders. It's not only good for your shoulders because it offers a reverse rotation of freestyle, but also because your body position is 180° opposite to when you swim freestyle, breaststroke, or butterfly.

Not only will swimming backstroke help keep your shoulders healthy, it will also improve your feel of the water. Swimming all the stroke variations will do this, but backstroke specifically will develop your latissimus dorsi strength and make it easier to improve your early vertical forearm catch in freestyle! Now that I've convinced you to swim a little bit more backstroke in every workout, let's get into the stroke mechanics!

Head Position

When breaking down any of the competitive strokes, we'll start with head position. We know that in order to swim faster, we must reduce drag and increase propulsion. In backstroke, the ideal head position is neutral and in-line with our spine. You need to be comfortable floating on your back on the surface of the water.

Your eyes should be looking straight up at the ceiling or sky, and your belly button should be at the surface level of the water. The simple biggest mistake swimmers make is tilting their head forward and looking down at your feet. When you tilt or lift your head up, your hips sink immediately. This shift in body position is even more dramatic than in freestyle.

The best backstrokers in the world can swim with a water bottle resting flat on their forehead even during a race. If you haven't tried this drill already, I highly encourage it. The next time you're at the pool, grab a water bottle or cup and fill it half way full with water. Rest it on your forehead and slowly start kicking. Once you have found balance while kicking on your back, start taking arm strokes.

Does the cup fall off your head??

You don't have to be a world-class swimmer to master this skill. In fact, I think any swimmer can swim a full 25 meters of backstroke with a cup half filled with water on their forehead.

You'll be able to master this after a few attempts if you're comfortable floating on your back first. I hope you can master this skill, and if you're not there yet, keep practicing.

The idea of swimming with a cup filled with water on your head is less about theatrics and more about swimming with a level head position. Our head position leads our body position, and we want to swim with as neutral of a body line as possible in the water.

Some swimmers are able to balance the cup on their forehead and still have poor head position. How is this possible? You can keep your forehead level, but your overall head position is too high out of the water. You want nearly your entire head submerged under the water.

70-80% of your head should be under the surface of the water. Your ears should be underwater as well, and only your face should be dry. Just like Freestyle, in backstroke you will be displacing the most water with your head first, which is why it's so important to keep it inline with your spine and the rest of your body.

Body Position

If you think about the part of your body that displaces the most water, it's your torso. After your head breaks the surface of the water and creates the most resistance, your shoulders, chest, and back follow.

Keeping with the theme of floating on top of the water and your head being inline with your spine, your legs should do the same. Because your hips and legs are narrower than your midsection and torso, it's important to maintain a low profile in the water.

This means minimizing the size of your kick and as you rotate, which we'll discuss soon, you must stay inline with your spine. Similarly to freestyle, the amplitude of your kick should be less than half a meter. The total distance between your toes and heels should be within your body line.

When you swim backstroke, your legs should be almost straight, and your toes should be pointed. The goal is generate some level of propulsion for the stroke but only while keeping a profile small enough to not increase total drag. In the last chapter on freestyle, I advised de-emphasizing the flutter kick.

In backstroke, this still holds true but to a lesser°. In freestyle, you can pull slightly more water per stroke and obtain an early vertical forearm with more leverage sooner than in the backstroke pull. Therefore, in freestyle you're less dependent on the kick to generate rotational momentum. In backstroke, because all these components are slightly less impactful, you do need a strong kick to help drive propulsion.

In freestyle, you can swim pretty fast without kicking and just dragging your legs. In backstroke, that's not going to work as well, and you'll suffer by not having a consistent driver of rotational momentum that the kick provides for. Just remember when you're kicking in backstroke, to keep it short, fast, and within your body line to not increase overall body drag.

The Pull

While the biggest similarities in freestyle and backstroke are head and body position, the largest difference between these long-axis strokes is how your arms catch and pull water under the surface and also how you recover your arms on top of the water.

When you start the catch phase of the stroke, your hand should enter the water pinkie finger first. Your arm should be 100% straight. From your shoulder to your middle finger should be as straight as a meter-stick. In contrast with freestyle, you recover with a bent elbow.

Similarly to freestyle, you should aim to enter the water at about shoulder width. Using the arms of the clock as a reference this would be 1 o'clock and 11 o'clock. Pro tip: you should actually feel like you're entering the water with your pinkie at 2 o'clock and 10 o'clock for a slightly wider hand entry. The reason for this is that most swimmers have a hard time judging where shoulder-width is and end up entering the water behind their head which is far too narrow.

Once your pinkie finger enters the water, you begin to drive that pinkie finger down towards the bottom of the pool, and after the entire hand is submerged you begin to sweep your hand so that your palm faces your feet. As you rotate your body and your hands get deeper, you should aim to have your forearm straight from your middle finger all the way to your elbow. At this point, your bent elbow should resemble the freestyle early vertical forearm, only, you'll be leaning towards your side, rather than on your stomach.

Once the catch is initiated, you pull the water by pushing your hand towards your hips with your palm and forearm leading the power. At this point, your opposite arm should have already exited the water. As you exit the water with your pulling hand, you should aim to finish the stroke with your thumb facing up as it leaves the water.

With your thumb pointing up, your arms should be straight out of the water and now, you'll be in the recovery phase of the stroke. This motion is symmetrical on both sides of your body.

In other words, when your right arm is under the water in the pull phase, your left arm is out of the water in the recovery phase. It should almost feel like your arms are a windmill. There is no pause at any point in the stroke.

A great drill to work on catching the water is swimming double arm backstroke.

DOUBLE-ARM BACKSTROKE DRILL

To execute this drill, simply float on your back and take both arm strokes at the same time. This drill is great for learning how to balance on your back at all phases of the stroke as well as entering the water at 11 o'clock and 1 o'clock with your pinky first. The most impactful part of this drill is, once your hands enter the water, being able to generate twice as much underwater force by pulling your hands at the same time.

When you do this double arm backstroke drill, it's critical that you do not rest your arms at the finish of the pull. As soon as you're done with the pull phase of the stroke, you should focus on exiting the water with your thumbs first as soon as possible to maintain forward momentum and stroke continuity. Additionally, this drill completely disregards any rotation in favor of focusing on swimming flat to focus on pulling with a shallow catch. We'll talk about rotation next!

Rotation

Just as in freestyle, when you swim backstroke you rotate side to side with rotational momentum generated from your hips. You can swim backstroke completely flat, but it will reduce the amount of water you can pull and make you tired much more quickly. In order to rotate effectively, you must start with a neutral body position and drive the rotation with your lower body.

Your hips drive the rotation, and your upper body simply follows. You should aim to rotate up to 45° to each side when swimming casual backstroke. The more you increase tempo, the less you'll be able to rotate. The best swimmers are able to maintain an effective° of rotation while increasing tempo for different distances and effort levels of backstroke.

A great drill to work on rotational momentum and also balance is 3 strokes + 12 kicks. This is the same drill that can be done for freestyle, but when you swim backstroke, you are able to breath the entire time because you're on your back. After taking three strokes, pause rotation on your side for 12 full kicks. This will teach you how to balance on your side. Then on the final kick, initiate rotation with your hips to start the three arm strokes.

While you do this drill, focus on rotating during the three strokes between the 12 kicks. When you pause for the kicks, remain on your side and keep your eyes up maintaining a neutral head position. When you swim backstroke normally, you will not pause all the way on your side, but the point of the drill is to build comfort and exaggerate this motion.

The more you swim backstroke, the more natural this rotation will feel. Eventually, you'll be in a position where it will be difficult to swim backstroke without rotating side to side just because your body will have become accustomed to moving forward with the help of rotational momentum.

Tempo

I could write an entire chapter just on tempo and how it applies to each of the four competitive strokes and swimming in general. But to keep things concise, I added tempo to this chapter, because swimming backstroke with a slow tempo is the single biggest detterent of success. This is most true for competitive swimmers looking to swim faster in backstroke and the Individual Medley.

The challenge we all face when swimming backstroke is the concept of being on our back and the opportunity to breathe whenever we choose. Now I should clarify; when we swim backstroke, there is actually a breathing pattern that follows your arm cadence. In other words, you take about one breath per arm cycle naturally, so if you move your arms faster, then the time between breaths becomes shorter. Keep in mind, moving your arms faster, also takes more energy, so your breathing/stroke tempo balances out.

When we swim backstroke, we can get lazy. I'm very guilty of this. When you train with a slower arm tempo, it's very difficult to increase this when it comes time to race. Increasing our backstroke tempo feels extremely exhausting and unsustainable. This is why it's so important to focus on your tempo when swimming backstroke. Don't let it get too slow. If it always feels too easy, you're probably not moving your arms fast enough. If you want to race fast, you need to train fast! It's that easy.

Let's go!!!

A great technique to work on increasing tempo in backstroke is called a "spin drill." This is where you do short bursts of spinning your arms in the backstroke motion as quickly as possible. In order to do this effectively, you'll need to break all conventional wisdom of body position we discussed in this chapter and position your body at a 45-90° angle to the water.

Your head and shoulders should be completely out of the water and your legs should be nearly a meter below the surface.

You have 10 seconds to spin your arms in this position as quickly as possible. The goal is not to make forward progress by pulling as much water as you can, rather increase your tempo to max speed. This is a high intensity and effort drill, so give yourself some rest between reps. After a few of these high effort bursts, you'll notice how much easier it is to swim backstroke with a higher tempo.

That's the goal! Swim more quickly with less effort. If you can train your body to swim backstroke with a higher average tempo while still maintaining distance per stroke, you'll be well on your way to swimming backstroke faster and smarter than ever before!

CHAPTER SEVEN

Breaststroke

AT ONE POINT IN HISTORY, Breaststroke was the most common stroke used for fitness swimmers and in competition! Breaststroke was the fastest style of swimming until the 20th century. To this day, you'll see many swimmers use this style as their primary stroke. This is mostly true in Asia and other parts of the world.

This is no surprise, because Breaststroke can be the most enjoyable and natural strokes to swim for some. For others, it's quite the opposite and breaststroke feels painfully slow. Advances in stroke technique over the last 200 years have allowed the other competitive strokes to zip by breaststroke in speed and efficiency.

Today, breaststroke is by far the slowest of the four competitive swimming strokes. While that might sound depressing, it shouldn't be. Breaststroke is an incredibly calming way to move through the water. In open-water swimming, it can be used as a way to temporarily relax and spot for direction. In an emergency, it's the easiest stroke to swim while continuously keeping your head out of the water to see what's ahead.

Recall that breaststroke and butterfly are both short-axis strokes. Rather than rotating around a center axis that extends from the head through the spine, in butterfly and backstroke you pivot the upper part of your body using your hips as a horizontal axis point.

Simply put, this upper body pivot in short-axis strokes and the fact that your body position is lower in the water is why breaststroke is the slowest stroke. This is no reason to be afraid of or avoid breaststroke. If anything, this means there's an even greater opportunity to advance your skills and swim faster because there is so much opportunity for improvement.

Body Position

Since we know that when we swim breaststroke we're lower in the water, we must first address our body's position. During the breath, your hips naturally sink to the lowest position of the stroke causing a massive amount of water resistance and therefore slowing you down.

The more effectively you can keep your hips high in the water, the less you'll slow down and the faster you'll swim. Remember, streamline is the fundamental body position in swimming. In breaststroke, every stroke starts and ends in this position. We'll discuss timing in the next section, but remember that your goal in breaststroke is to keep your body position as high as possible during all phases of the stroke.

When you watch someone swim breaststroke from the side of the pool, it's easy to see only their head come out of the water every time they take a breath. Unlike the other competitive strokes, sometimes this is all you see. In backstroke, butterfly, and freestyle, you will see the swimmers arms recover over the surface of the water, and sometimes a large part of the torso comes out of the water.

If only your head comes out of the water in breaststroke, that means your head is no longer inline with your spine. When you swim breaststroke, you want to imagine a laser from the center of the top of your head that runs through your spine to your hips. You can't bend lasers, so remember when you lift your upper body to take a breath, this laser must remain in a straight line.

This laser analogy ends at your hips. Your hips to your toes must remain as close to the surface of the water as possible at all points of the stroke. When you return to streamline after the breath, the laser will start at the top of your head and extend all the way to your toes. This flat body position is the fastest phase of the stroke and in the next section we'll discuss how to get there!

Timing

I'll make this very simple. Every time that you swim breaststroke, say in your head:

1. Pull
2. Kick
3. Glide

That's the breaststroke timing. It's that easy. You might ask yourself, when do you breathe??

You breathe during the first phase of the stroke, the pull! As you start to pull, you lift your head up to breath. By the time you've taken a breath and your arms begin to recover back to streamline, you enter the second phase of the stroke. The kick drives your body into streamline and the final phase of the stroke.

The fastest part of breaststroke is the transition from the second phase to the third phase. When you finish the kick and extend into streamline for the glide, you carry the most speed. This is the fastest part of the stroke by far and results in forward propulsion. No matter how strong your pull is, you will not be able to master breaststroke without an effective kick and glide.

For myself and many others, the glide is the most enjoyable and satisfying part of the stroke. It's the fruits of labor from the first and second phase. If you had a strong pull and kick, you'll be able to have an amazing glide. The length of the glide really depends on how long and fast you're swimming breaststroke.

For more casual swimming, the glide might be a full second in streamline. In a short 25-meter maximum effort sprint, the glide phase may only be a tenth of a second. The duration of the glide dictates the stroke tempo. No the other way around. Swimmers often try to swim faster by increasing stroke tempo and neglecting the glide phase. This is a mistake. You can't skip one part of the stroke.

If you watch the fastest swimmers in the world, the stroke mechanics are virtually the same in the 50, 100, and 200 meter distances. The major difference comes in how long the glide phase is maintained between strokes. In a 50-meter sprint, this might be one or two tenths of a second. In the 100-meter race, this might extend to three or four tenths of a second. In a 200-meter race, elite swimmers can hold their streamlines for nearly a full second before starting the next stroke.

When it comes to stroke timing, this is most important in breaststroke. You simply can't be "off". It just doesn't work. Pull, kick, glide. Repeat after me: Pull, Kick, Glide. Good.

Every time you swim breaststroke, you need to say this in your head. A great way to reinforce this concept of elongating the stroke is to simply count how many strokes it takes you to swim across the pool.

Count how many strokes you take in a 25 or 50-meter pool. Then, try again and take one less stroke. Then take off another stroke. For simplicity, count every breath as a stroke. If you count 12 strokes for your 25-meter breaststroke swim, then try again and take 11, then 10. At a certain point, you'll sacrifice speed and momentum for the sake of reducing total stroke count.

There is a fine balance between maximizing distance per stroke and speed. Recall the swimming equation for how these variables work with each other. This balance in stroke length and efficiency will become easier to manage as you practice counting strokes.

I personally count how many strokes I take every length I swim breaststroke. I generally swim six strokes comfortably in a 25-meter pool. If I want to stretch it out, I'll take five strokes. If I'm increasing my tempo in favor of speed, I'll take seven. It's not perfect, but it's definitely routine, and this allows me to practice patience and discipline to always maximize distance per stroke. I encourage you to do the same in not only breaststroke but all the other strokes as well!

. . .

Pull

Now that we understand when to perform the different parts of breaststroke, we need to talk about how each phase works. The first part of the stroke is our pull. It initiates from the streamline position. As you separate your hands from streamline, you'll sweep out slightly. Your hands should sweep just past your shoulders and position your upper body to rise out of the water for the breath.

At this point, you'll pull your hands towards your chest pulling yourself forward. In the middle of the pull phase, you should focus on initiating an early vertical forearm with both arms simultaneously. Unlike the other strokes, the duration of this EVF is short lived because you must bring your hands together to return to streamline. Once the pulling motion is complete, it's imperative to return your hands to streamline as quickly as possible to reduce the amount of drag you create.

During the recovery phase of the stroke, you're actually pushing yourself backwards. This is why it's so important to do this swiftly, and I encourage swimmers to keep the hands at the surface level of the water. Your thumbs should skim over the surface and drive your hands forward as if you're handing someone a plate with both hands.

Unlike the other strokes, the pull in breaststroke has a legal restriction on how it should be performed correctly. This sounds technical, but it really is not. In breaststroke, when you pull underwater, your hands can not cross below your belly button before recovering back to streamline.

This is a mistake beginner swimmers make often because of the feeling of immediate speed and power when you pull both of your arms down at the same time. The problem with this movement is not only that you will be disqualified if done in a competition, but it's actually slower than if you made your pull smaller.

It sounds counterintuitive: pull less water and swim more quickly?

Yes! This is because the increase in propulsion to pull your arms down further is negated by the greater resistance in recovering your hands back to streamline. Therefore, the ideal distance to pull your hands down is to your nose. If you're pulling your hands past your nose, it's too far.

Remember the timing: Pull, Kick Glide. Your goal should be to finish the pull phase, kick your hands forward to streamline in as little time as possible. This is the slowest phase of the stroke, so it's important that it's done swiftly while maintaining an efficient stroke technique.

Kick

There are two kinds of people in the world. Those who have a natural breaststroke kick, and those who do not. The "natural" breaststrokers are comfortable flexing their feet, treading water with an egg beater or frog kick, and often walk a little funny with their feet pointing out. If this sounds like you, you have a leg up (pun intended) for swimming breaststroke. I myself fall into this category as well.

It's not all sunshine and roses for us "breaststrokers"! We often struggle at pointing our toes for flutter and dolphin kicks and as a result are poor at kicking in freestyle, backstroke, and butterfly. If you don't feel comfortable flexing your feet and have trouble with the frog kick, you're like most swimmers!

Regardless of which group you're in, everyone can always improve their breaststroke kick. Even if you're a very beginner, by working on the right elements of the kick and focusing on some key drills, you can improve your efficiency and power in breaststroke. This second phase of the stroke is so important it's often cited by world class swimmers as being 70-80% of the propulsive power in the stroke.

Without an effective kick, it's really difficult to swim breaststroke fast. The best drill to work on improving your kicking technique, speed, power, and efficiency is called "heel tag." It's relatively simple to execute and will do wonders for beginner and advanced swimmers.

Heel tag:

Start on your back and place your hands at your side underneath your butt as if you're handcuffed. You want your hands to rest directly under your bottom with your palms facing down to the bottom of the pool. While floating on your back, begin the breaststroke kick by bringing your heels back to touch your hands. Your feet should be flexed at this point, and you should focus on using your hamstrings to bring your heels back towards your bottom.

The key with this first part of the kick is to keep your knees under the surface of the water while also keeping your knees relatively close together. You should not have your knees separate wider than your shoulders by the time your heels touch your palms. For most people, this is about half a meter in width.

Once your heels touch your palms, now you begin the propulsive phase of the kick! With your feet flexed, bring your feet back together using the bottoms of your feet to "pull" the water until your ankles touch each other. At the end of the kick phase, you should point your toes and glide. Similarly to the different phases to the overall breaststroke stroke, when you kick, you should have a glide at the end of each kick repetition.

An easy way to understand the kick timing is to say to yourself: up, out, around, and together. That is the entire timing of the breaststroke kick. Bring your heels "up" to your butt, then bring your heels "out" by laterally rotating your heels just outside your body-line, then bring your heels back "around and together" back to the starting position. Think to yourself, "up, out, around, and together" every time you go through the kick motion in this drill.

This drill can also be done on your stomach. The only thing that complicates this movement is the breathing. Simply insert a breath before starting the motion, so the timing becomes: Breath, up, out, around, and together. There should be a moment to glide before taking the next breath to repeat the cycle.

Another variation of this drill to focus on kick technique is holding your arms in a streamline position while you float on your back or stomach.

The only difference with this variation is you'll no longer be able to touch your heels to your hands and instead rely on your vestibular awareness to bring your heels back far enough. Kicking in streamline on your back is the best way to train the breaststroke kick over longer durations while improving technique. Just be sure to keep your knees under the surface of the water the best you can when kicking on your back in streamline.

Pullout

I was debating adding this section to the chapter because the breaststroke pullout has evolved so much in the last two decades. Today, elite swimmers are traveling a full 15 meters underwater off the wall in every length of a breaststroke race. It's incredible to watch but frustrating if you don't know how to do it.

Let's backup, what is a breaststroke pullout?

A pullout is something that's performed only in breaststroke —when you push off the wall or dive in for a start. It's used to maintain momentum from the wall or dive and carry more speed into the first full stroke over the water.

It's performed by starting in a streamline position. This is how you should push off the wall every time you start a length of any stroke, but in breaststroke, you're legally allowed to do a full stroke underwater before surfacing. The way this works is after you begin to feel yourself slowing down in the streamline position, you take a full arm pull bringing your hands down to your hips.

Once you begin to slow down in this position, you then bring your hands back to streamline and take one kick before starting a full breaststroke stroke over the water. At any point during the underwater phase, you can also take one dolphin kick to help propel yourself forward. The best swimmers in the world usually do this before separating their hands in stream-line to initiate the pull down.

This may sound a bit tricky, so I encourage you to refer to the complementary online course videos to see it in action. It's really important in all phases of the breaststroke pullout to focus on reducing drag. The goal of a pullout is to maintain your speed off the wall or dive. You'll never generate more propulsive power from the pullout than when you dove in the water or pushed off the wall.

This is something to keep in mind when focusing on improving your pullout. The goal is maintenance of speed versus generating new speed. Surely the dolphin kick and arm pull down will create propulsion, but that's designed to keep you moving underwater. This is how some of the best swimmers in the world are able to travel 15 meters underwater before taking a single stroke on top of the water.

Training

When we put it all together, there are a lot of areas to improve in breaststroke. From mastering the timing, pull, kick, and streamline there are a lot of opportunities to improve regardless of how fast or proficient you already are. Beyond mastering the stroke mechanics, there is massive potential to swim faster just by being smarter with your training.

In the short axis strokes, it's paramount to swim with a high body position, with proper stroke technique, and at a high intensity. This is less true for freestyle and backstroke because you can still swim those two strokes "easy" and not sacrifice stroke timing and technique. Breaststroke is a beast on its own and should be treated as such in training.

Specifically, focus on training with fantastic stroke length and intensity at all times in breaststroke. This applies to butterfly as well, and we'll discuss this more in the next chapter. When choosing a workout or creating your own for breaststroke, I'd recommend giving preference to shorter distances with higher repetitions and increased rest. For example, rather than swimming a 300 breaststroke continuously, break it up into 6 x 50s.

Rather than swimming 6 x 50s with only 5 seconds rest, swim those same 6 x 50s with 15-20 seconds rest. Give yourself the opportunity to swim a little bit faster, with more power per stroke, and give yourself the appropriate rest needed to do so. Think about swimming sets that are Ultra Short Race Pace Training (USRPT). This is a style where you swim high repeat counts of a shorter distance at race pace. More on this in the FAQs at the end of the book.

When it comes to swimming a faster breaststroke, just remember that the goal is always to perform the stroke with optimal stroke technique at intensities that simulate a desired result. Often, this is easiest to execute when the stroke is broken up into different parts. For example, swimming sets that target different parts of the stroke like the kick or pull in order to focus on executing these stroke elements with more impact.

If your goal is leisure swimming and you're not concerned with how fast it takes you to get to the end of the pool, then don't worry so much about training at race pace. However, breaking up the stroke into different parts to train is still a great way to improve the kick, pull, and timing of the stroke for swimmers of all levels!

CHAPTER EIGHT

Butterfly

BUTTERFLY IS one of the most difficult strokes to master and probably the most tiring of all the competitive strokes. There's a few reasons for this that we'll get into in this chapter, but the goal is not to simply swim butterfly for survival. I want you to thrive when you swim butterfly!!

Swimming butterfly with an efficient stroke requires extra energy and advanced technique knowledge. If you're new to butterfly, it might feel impossible! But trust me, it's not. I'm going to break down the basics of the stroke and share my favorite drills to help you perfect your technique and swim faster!

Even if you're more experienced in butterfly, you'd be surprised just how much you can improve by reinforcing some of the fundamental skills in your technique. Butterfly is a relatively "new" stroke, so we are always learning and adapting to innovations in technique and training!

You're saying butterfly is new?

Yes! Butterfly was developed in the 1930s as a style of swimming breaststroke. A few innovative swimmers realized that they could swim breaststroke faster if they recovered their arms over the water. After just a few years of this, more and more swimmers started to recover their arms forward above the water and the swimming term 'butterfly' – was born.

By 1956, Butterfly became an official race in the Olympic Games hosted in Melbourne, and the rest is history! As you can see, butterfly is new, innovative, and will continue to evolve for decades to come! Let's explore how you can swim butterfly faster and smarter than ever before!

FLOW

Have you ever been completely immersed in something you're doing? Oblivious to the outside world, your only focus is on the progress you're making on what you're doing right then and there! Maybe you've been doing something you love, like playing the piano, walking in nature, or maybe even swimming. It's like you're in a different world, a different dimension!

This surreal experience is called "flow" in the world of psychology. Flow is one of life's highly enjoyable states of being; when we're immersed in the present. Our mind and body are fully engaged in what we're doing. When we swim, this is our aspired state of mind and body.

In order to achieve it, we must be willing and able to connect our entire body to the water. This couldn't be more true than when we swim butterfly. It is truly a total body experience, and in order to feel a state of "flow" in the water, we must focus on connecting to the water.

How might we do this, you might ask.

With "Flow drill," of course! This is my favorite drill for butterfly and improving underwater dolphin kick. It engages the entire body from finger tips to toes while also stimulating the mind.

FLOW DRILL

In order to perform this drill, start by pushing off the wall in a Superman position on your stomach with your arms extended and on the surface of the water.

Superman flies with his hands fisted. But for this drill, you'll want your hands open and fingertips at the surface of the water. Use your upper body to press your chest down allowing your hips to rise up above the water. Your face is looking down, and the goal of the drill is to mimic a dolphin motion on the surface of the water. Your head should remain on the surface of the water with your eyes looking down.

Your body should look like a sine curve on a graph, oscillating up and down equally. Although most of the forward momentum is being generated by your chest and hips moving up and down, this motion actually starts with your palms and extends to your toes. Focus on using every centimeter of musculature of your body including the top of your diaphragm down through your hip flexors and quads.

Don't forget that the dolphin motion has an up and down force, meaning you'll need to engage musculature on your backside as well including your lower back, glutes, and hamstrings. This is the fundamental body position in butterfly. When you need to breathe, lift your head up, or use a snorkel. Using fins helps a lot to really feel forward progress with this drill. Engage your entire body, and find your flow!

. . .

Pull

Now that you have the body rhythm down, it's time we discuss what your arms should be doing! Without overcomplicating the stroke, think of the pull phase of the butterfly stroke as two freestyle strokes happening at the same time. Your arms and hands should be directly in front of your shoulders at the start of the pull.

As you press your chest forward and down, you'll catch the water with your hand, forearm, and upper part of your arm. Your goal is to achieve an early vertical forearm with both arms simultaneously. Anchor the water with your hands and forearms and pull yourself forward.

There are two core differences between the butterfly pull and a freestyle pull.

Difference 1: The first core difference is the rotational momentum that occurs in freestyle. When you extend your arm in freestyle, your body is rotated slightly to the side of the arm that's extended. Then, the pull initiates and follows in the same line as your shoulder with rotation. When you swim butterfly, there is no rotation, so your pull pattern will naturally be different.

When you swim butterfly, you should try to maintain your arms at shoulder width throughout the pull phase underwater. Naturally, as you finish the stroke, your hands and arms will come in closer to your body so that you exit the water with your hands fully extended at your side. At this point, your hands are past your waist and the goal is to keep your arms as straight as possible on the recover phase.

Difference 2: The second core difference between the pull in freestyle and butterfly is the timing and power of the stroke. In freestyle, you have a bit more leniency in how long it takes to initiate an early vertical forearm and just how fast you pull your arm through the water. In butterfly, on the other hand, the pull needs to be more explosive and calculated.

There's no such thing as a "slow butterfly pull." This really throws off the timing of the stroke and makes your technique much less efficient. Instead, focus on pulling with power. As soon as you initiate the catch, your goal is to accelerate your hands and arms to the finish of the pull phase. The over-water recovery phase of the stroke should be controlled and relaxed.

When you recover your arms, focus on keeping your hands relaxed. Your arms are straight and gracefully stretch over the water like a bird flying just above the surface hunting for its prey. I once heard the expression "angel arms" from a coach when instructing younger swimmers on how to recover the arms in butterfly. I like this visualization because it creates a calming mood for what should be a controlled and calculated phase of the stroke!

Butterfly Kick

The mechanics of the dolphin kick and timing of how the kick(s) align with the butterfly stroke is very challenging for most beginner swimmers. Ideally, your timing and body rhythm leads the body-line, and you don't have to over think how you kick in butterfly.

In the next chapter, we will discuss the underwater dolphin kick in great detail. As a baseline, remember what I shared about flow—a total body connection to the water. You want to undulate through the water, and the kick in butterfly is truly a total body movement that starts with the upper abs and extends through the diaphragm, finishing at the toes.

When you swim butterfly, there are two kicks for every stroke. This means that there is a kick at the start of the pull and another kick at the end of the pull. There are a few different ways you can think about this that will help in timing this in your head. One way to describe this is by thinking about kicking your arms forward in the stroke and then kicking your hands as you finish the pull.

Ideally, both kicks should be similar in power and size. Naturally, one will be larger just based on the mechanics of the stroke. Another way to think about how you timing the kick with your arm pulls is to simply only focus on one of the kicks. Focus on the kick that allows you to bring your arms around to the front and press your chest down. This downward press of your chest brings your hips up naturally.

BUTTERFLY KICK DRILL

A great drill to time the body motion and kicks in butterfly is by swimming single arm butterfly. During this drill, you'll breath to your side with an almost-freestyle lille arm recovery. Focus on pressing your chest down as your arm comes around. By focusing on just one stroke, and swimming slightly to your side with a freestyle-type arm recovery, it will make it much easier to feel the body rhythm of butterfly.

Your opposite arm should be held in a neutral streamline position while the other arm is taking strokes. Give it a shot with shorter distances and alternate arms every two or three strokes. This is a great drill that can be incorporated in butterfly training. This can be done by alternating 25s or 50s with this drill and the full butterfly stroke.

Breathing

So how do you breathe?

I've seen swimmers with incredible butterfly stroke mechanics swim at near world-record speed, until they take a breath. The greatest of all time, Michael Phelps was known for breathing every single stroke in all of his butterfly races. This makes sense. When you breathe, you have to lift your head up, which drops your body position and disrupts the stroke.

This can all be minimized dramatically if your timing and stroke mechanics are correct. If you're off on the timing, then taking a breath will feel like a chore. Ideally, you take the breath right as you initiate the catch phase with your hands and an early vertical forearm position. Lift your face out of the water looking forward and try to keep your chin right at the surface of the water.

Keep in mind, when you breathe, you only need to lift your head high enough to make a clear path for air to enter through your mouth. Lifting your head too high or holding your head for too long out of the water will cause your hips to sink and lose forward momentum. You should leave your chin above the surface of the water through the duration of the pull phase. Then, as you begin to recover your arms, lower your chin and face back under the surface.

Your head should return to the neutral body line position with your eyes looking at the bottom of the pool by the time you finish the recovery phase. As your head lowers into the water, you'll want to press your chest down to raise your hips up. A great drill to focus on this timing is a drill I like to "best balance distance."

Best Balance Distance Drill

This drill is performed in the neutral "flow" body line. Your arms are extended above your head floating on the surface of the water. You start by taking three dolphin kicks. Then, on the third dolphin kick, initiate an arm pull and take a breath. Rather than swimming continuous butterfly, you pause your arm movement to re-calibrate in the neutral flow position between strokes. Three dolphin kicks, then 1 stroke and a breath, and repeat!

Focus on the timing of the pull in relation to the breath and dolphin kicks. Each stroke cycle is an opportunity to rehearse this. I recommend only doing this in increments of 25 or 50 meters with plenty of rest to feel fresh for each attempt.

Training

Similar to breaststroke, butterfly is a short axis stroke! There is no rotational momentum like in freestyle and backstroke, and therefore, proper mechanics and timing become critical at every speed of the stroke. When we train butterfly, it must be done with a focus on keeping a high body posture in the water at close to race pace.

This doesn't mean sprinting butterfly all the time in workout. That would lead to extreme stroke fatigue and you wouldn't be able to swim more than 100 or 200 meters in a single workout session. Instead, focus on swimming butterfly with easy speed. You want to feel like you're moving quickly with great stroke fundamentals without taxing your body's energy reserves.

EASY SPEED BUTTERFLY DRILL

The easiest way to achieve this "easy speed" approach is by swimming shorter distances of butterfly. Rather than swim a 200m butterfly straight, swim 4 x 50s or 8 x 25s. Give yourself adequate rest and train your body to swim shorter distances, averaging a faster speed. This can also be done by alternating butterfly with freestyle.

To create a more aerobic impact, rather than swimming a 5 x 100s butterfly, instead swim 5 x 200s alternating 50 butterfly, 50 freestyle. This will result in 500 meters of butterfly in total in a 1,000 meter set. This concept of breaking apart the training into more manageable segments is how the best swimmers in the world train short-axis strokes.

A great drill that focuses on developing a more powerful butterfly stroke is swimming butterfly with a freestyle kick. Butterfly pull with freestyle kick reinforces the underwater power phase of the stroke and actually flattens the stroke to promote a higher tempo. I love doing this drill with fins for added propulsion. Just like any drill, do it in moderation, over shorter distances to ensure proper form and prevent over-fatigue.

Butterfly is an extremely taxing stroke on your body. It's a great workout and requires a high level of mental and physical engagement. Don't be intimidated by the challenge. Instead, embrace it and become one with the water. Find your flow and swim like a dolphin. In the next chapter, we'll dive into how you can master your flow and swim like a dolphin under the water!

CHAPTER NINE

The 5th Stroke

UNDERWATER STREAMLINE IS CONSIDERED to be the 5th stroke of swimming! It is absolutely the fastest way for a human to move through the water – even faster than swimming freestyle.

When you watch the Olympics on TV, you'll see all the top athletes dolphin kick underwater almost 15m off the start and after every turn. It's a dolphin, it's a sailfish, it's Michael Phelps surging ahead of the competition with incredible underwater speed!

In short course swimming (25-yard or 25-meter pools), the underwater streamline push off the start and every turn makes up approximately two thirds of the entire race. Even if you're not a competitive swimmer, recognize that by improving your underwater dolphin kick and streamline off the wall you'll be able to carry more speed into the swimming phase of each lap.

Remember that the fastest part of the length is when you dive in or push off the wall. The rest of the time you're decelerating so you may as well carry as much speed as possible from an underwater streamline into your first stroke.

Aquatic Prowess

Like anything in life, if you want to be the best at something, look at what the best are currently doing. If we apply this to underwater swimming, we might look at top swimmers like Michael Phelps or Natalie Caughlin. Both dominated their competition and made headlines for how impressive their underwater streamlines were.

If we take an even higher level view on the concept of underwater swimming, we should look beyond the human race. If we truly want to learn from the best, we must look to our aquatic friends under the surface: Fish. In essence, fish are the most efficient creatures through water because the water is their home!

A Black Marlin can reach a top speed of 129 kilometers per hour underwater! It's amazing to think that a fish can move at highway driving speeds underwater. The Black Marlin has to propel itself through a medium of resistance that's 800x more dense than air. Incredible!

The Black Marlin is not alone! Sailfish have been clocked at 109 kilometers per hour and swordfish can reach up to 100 kilometers per hour. Even Penguins, which are technically considered birds, can reach speeds of up to 35 kilometers per hour underwater.

The fastest humans can streamline kick up to 10 kilometers per hour underwater which is approximately 2.5 meters per second. That's blazing but still less than one tenth the speed of our aquatic friends. Underwater streamline truly is the 5th stroke. How is this possible, and what can we learn from our aquatic friends to be more fish-like underwater?

Marine Physics

Think of your body as a sine wave, a mathematical curve that illustrates a smooth periodic oscillation. If you follow the curve through the origin of a graph, it goes up and down in a smooth motion. In a perfect world, the oscillation is even both above and below the x-axis.

If you watch a dolphin or any fish swim underwater, what appears to be a wiggle motion is actually an equally balanced oscillation to create forward propulsion. In this analogy think of the amplitude of the oscillation as the total size of your dolphin kick. When you kick both underwater and in all the applicable strokes, focus on kicking in both directions.

Even if you can kick with a perfectly symmetrical dolphin kick, you'll still be much slower than a fish casually swimming through the water. So, why is this?

Well, for starters, we as humans are not built perfectly symmetrically to be able to produce an even dolphin or flutter kick. A fish, on the other hand, can have an even up-and-down or side-to-side propulsion motion. When we think about this from a physics perspective, it makes sense.

Not only is the fish symmetrical or at least more-symmetrical, but a fish uses its entire frame length to create propulsion. A fish is able to apply pressure at every point of its frame length. As humans, we're built with stiff bones and relatively inflexible body parts.

We only have three major points of inflection to create propulsion with our bodies. We have our hips, which provide the largest pivot point of our body. Next, we have our knees, which provide a relatively poor pivot point for our lower body. Finally, we have our ankles, which like our knees, only bend in one direction.

We as humans are really only about 10-20% efficient in using our full frame length for dolphin kick. This explains why fish can swim up to 10x our speed underwater. This also explains why some of the best swimmers in the world can swim so quickly underwater. It's a combination of body awareness, technique, physical strength, and flexibility that allows some swimmers to move up to 10 kilometers per hour underwater.

Technique

Increasing your body's surface area to generate forward propulsion is the fundamental way to streamline faster underwater. Your goal should be to increase your frame's efficiency and apply more pressure with more surface area in both the up and down direction of the kick.

The amplitude of your kick refers to the total distance from the top of the kick curve to the bottom of the kick curve. In other words, the highest point your toes reach and lowest point your heels reach. This is the total water displacement of your underwater dolphin kick.

If your kick amplitude is big, then you'll get more propulsion but also increase the amount of drag you create. If your amplitude is too small, then you'll miss out on added propulsion. Everyone's kick amplitude is different depending on flexibility, body type, and general strength. Just keep in mind, you have less and less strength at the outer range of your kick amplitude.

In order to kick faster, you should focus on increasing your distance per kick while maintaining your kick tempo. This will happen when you increase your body's surface area creating the propulsion and also develop more strength. You might see top swimmers move their hands to initiate the underwater dolphin kick. In these instances, the hands are more like a stabilizer to elongate the body's frame. Power doesn't come from the hands, it comes from your rib cage down to the toes.

While this might sound complicated to develop and improve upon, it's really not. Here's three tips on how to balance the size of your kick, increase propulsion, and minimize resistance.

3 Tips To Improve

1. Focus on two-directional kicking

Unlike a fish, our frames are not symmetrical. It's much easier for us to walk forward than in reverse. We can kick a soccer ball in front of us much more easily than behind us. You get the picture. Because of this, we must think about and train our body to kick in both directions.

In one direction of the kick, we engage our abs, hip flexors, and quads. In the opposite direction, we use our lower back, glutes, and hamstrings. You can think of this second phase of the kick as the "recovery" portion of the kick only because it's the segment in time when we're re-positioning our body to the more powerful direction of the kick.

I'm hesitant to use the word "recovery" because you do, in fact, generate propulsion during this phase. Although you can not generate as much power, you do create a propulsive force that drives you forward. Beginners are generally only proficient in the phase of the kick that leverages the natural pivot strength of our hips, knees, and ankles. This part of the kick mimics kicking a soccer ball.

The best underwater kickers apply forward pressure in both directions of the kick. In training, you need to focus on the reverse of the powerful part of the kick in order to return more quickly to the more powerful part of the kick. The closer you can get to the symmetrical sine graph, the more evenly distributed your power will be and the faster you'll go underwater.

Focus on using your hips and not bending your knees too much. Your body should look like a dolphin underwater, not a struggling fifth-round pick soccer player underwater. Just keep your kick amplitude inline with the rest of your body, and you'll be swimming like a dolphin in no time!

2. Train the dolphin kick in all four planes of motion

The most creative and impactful way to train your under-water dolphin kick is to kick in different body positions. This means developing balance and technical proficiency kicking on your front, back, and sides. This can be done in streamline on your stomach with a snorkel or on your back in streamline.

Kicking in every body position will improve your body's feel of the water. The goal is to develop a fish-like sense of flow underwater. This can only be done by spending time awakening the acute nerve endings in your skin and engaging your body's musculature. The more muscle fibers you can engage doing drills where you kick in all four planes of motion, the more impactful your dolphin kick training will be.

I love doing these drills with fins. Flow drill on the surface of the water with fins and a snorkel is a fantastic way to develop a strong dolphin kick by focusing on engaging the core musculature. You can also kick on your side with one arm extended forward. This is a great drill for not only developing underwater dolphin kick but also the body motion for the butterfly stroke.

3. Increase flexibility, ankle mobility, and functional strength

Your body is a vessel! When you train different components of each stroke and technique, you improve the versatility of your vessel. The more refined you can become as an athlete in the water, the more you'll improve as a swimmer. This means improving flexibility, developing functional strength and overall body awareness in the water.

In the following sections, we'll discuss in more detail strength training out of the water, but just remember that improving your strength is just one component of developing a strong underwater dolphin kick. Consider your flexibility and technique as well to swim faster and smarter underwater.

Focus on kicking with your hips and training all four planes of motion. You'll see (and feel) the results after just a few sessions. We all aspire to swim underwater like our aquatic friends, so practice everyday, and you'll be swimming with the fish in no time.

MAIN SET II:

Out of the Water

INTRODUCTION

Swimming is more than just going back and forth in a lap pool until you get tired. It is more than swimming a 1,000-meter or 5,000-meter workout. It goes deeper than developing a feel for the water and building aerobic capacity in the water. To understand how to truly optimize your potential in the water, we need to approach swimming from a holistic perspective!

Holistic fitness includes what you do in the water as well as on land. It includes strength training, nutrition, recovery, and your mental mindset. In this section, we'll explore the out of water elements that contribute to our performance in the water. This approach will yield not only the best performance but also the most enjoyment. You'll also reduce your chances of injury so you can keep swimming later in life.

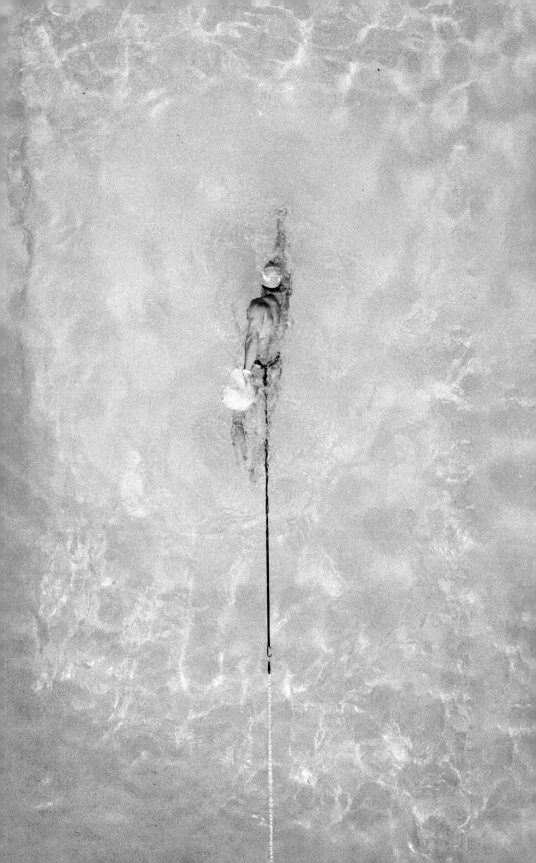

CHAPTER TEN

Strength Training

DID YOU SKIP LEG DAY?

Of course not!

Swimmers lift legs every single day!

We do?

Eh, sort of...

What does that even mean? If you're confused, this is how most swimmers feel when it comes to any sort of physical exercise out of the water. Fear not, this chapter is going to be highly informative! If you have done any workouts on land outside of the pool, you have a head start on most of the swimming population.

Swimmers have the unfortunate reputation of being clumsy and poorly balanced outside of the water. I would argue this used to be more true for anyone who grew up swimming before the year 2000. Since then, our fundamental understanding of training outside of the pool has advanced dramatically.

Today, we have a better understanding of human physiology

and strength training. This is one reason why more swimmers are faster today than 10 or 20 years ago. This is true for every age group. 18 year olds are faster than ever, and similarly, 58-year-olds continue to break masters world records.

Swimming is the fountain of youth! Whether you intend to swim well into your 90s or if you're more concerned with breaking a world record, in this chapter we're going to explore strength and conditioning, otherwise referred to as "dryland training."

What is dryland training, exactly?

To put it simply, dryland training (a.k.a. Strength and Conditioning) involves using your own bodyweight or equipment, like dumbbells or resistance bands, to develop muscle, strength, and power. If you're new to any of this, getting started might seem a little intimidating, but implementing strength training into your swimming routine will help in a massive way.

You can start with bodyweight exercises that require no equipment, are total body, and will give you a great workout. As you develop your balance, posture, and strength, you can increase your frequency of training and start to add equipment. Later in the chapter, I will share my top bodyweight exercises that require no equipment.

Why do dryland training?

Most forms of dryland training have numerous benefits for swimmers. The main motivation for many swimmers is the potential to increase performance. By building strength out of the water, you'll be able to apply this newfound herculean strength in the pool or open water to swim faster. Dryland training can develop your core strength, explosive power, and general aerobic fitness as well.

A less common but equally important reason to do dryland training is to prevent injury. We'll go deeper into this topic in the next chapter, but as a baseline, understand that overuse injuries are common in swimming. Dryland adds variety to your workouts and engages your muscles in different ways, which can realign your posture in the water and reduce your chances of injury.

Something I love about dryland training is how engaging it can be both physically and mentally. Doing the same or similar workouts in the pool can become monotonous. There's something about pushing your body on land that's different than doing it in the pool.

I also love dryland training because it's an opportunity to mix things up. It's like a breath of fresh air, literally! You can avoid burnout by mixing up your training and doing creative dryland workouts to stay mentally on top of your workout routine.

Finally, if for whatever reason, if you don't have access to a pool to train in, you can still get in a great workout. Sometimes you're traveling, on a tight schedule, or there's a global pandemic that has shut down all your local pools.

Regardless, no pool, no excuses!

Types of Dryland Training

Before we get into specific physiological movements, it's important to understand the different types of training you can do out of the water. Similarly to a swim workout, there are different variables that we can tweak to achieve a desired outcome. This includes the specific exercise, which is analogous to the type of stroke we swim.

There's also the duration of the activity, number of reps, and intensity of each specific set or rep. You can also manipulate the amount of rest you have between each set or repetition. All these variables contribute to the type of workout you will execute. A few major types are listed below:

- *Muscle Endurance Training:* This is a more beginner-friendly type of workout. You can start by lifting a higher volume, meaning more reps and sets, with lighter weights. This allows your tissues to build up tolerance for more intense training programs later. You can focus on technique rather than trying to add weight. Remember, you can't expect to make progress when you constantly have to stop because you're completely out of breath.
- *Circuit Training:* This involves going through a series of several exercises until you reach the last one, resting, and then repeating all the exercises again. Think of a circuit as a set group in a pool workout. Often, a circuit will run multiple rounds through with minimal or no rest between each exercise. You can modify this kind of workout to align with your specific strength goals. You can manipulate your work-to-rest ratio in circuits depending on what kind of training effect you're after.
- *Hypertrophy Training:* Strength training can be used to increase the size of your muscles. This type of training is the least useful for swimmers. You also

have to be lifting medium-to-high reps of a moderate to heavy weight consistently to see significant changes to the size of your muscles. In other words, dryland training a couple times a week isn't going to make you look massive. This is actually a good thing, because carrying around unnecessary muscle mass will only cause you to sink and slow you down in the water.

- *Max Strength Training:* This type of training is best transitioned to once you've built up your muscle endurance and mastered basic technique using your body weight. This kind of training involves bringing your number of repetitions down to about 3–6 and increasing the amount of resistance or weight you're moving.
- *Explosive Power Training:* Explosive power training is more advanced and not for beginners. This involves training at maximum intensity for short periods of time. Olympic lifts are the most common example of this. While many of these advanced movements are reserved for those who have a bit more experience in dryland training, this doesn't mean you can't train explosive power without weights.
- *Plyometrics:* also known as jump training or plyos, are exercises in which muscles exert maximum force in short intervals of time, with the goal of increasing power. Examples of this would include box jumps, jump squats, and plyo push ups!

These types of movements on land translate to the water well because you're able to move in an explosive way without the resistance of water. You can think of how pushing off the wall in streamline is similar to a burpee or a jump squat!

A big misconception by swimmers is that you need to mimic the major competitive strokes on land to gain strength in the water. This is not true, and while focusing on swimming specific movements and muscle groups can be beneficial, it shouldn't dominate your out of water strength training approach.

Instead of grabbing free weights and swinging your arms around to mimic backstroke, it's more important to focus on compound movements that engage your core! Compound exercises work multiple muscle groups at the same time. For example, a squat is a compound exercise that works the quadriceps, glutes, and calves.

When you perform a compound movement like a squat, your core is engaged in order to balance your weight through the movement. This is important in swimming because when you balance your body in the water, your core must be activated to maintain a high body position. Let's explore some "swimming specific" movements that can amplify this.

Swimming-Specific Movements

Swimming-specific movements focus on stability, flexibility, and strength. When you're just getting started, it's important to focus on compound exercises. This ensures you use the muscle groups that will be engaged when you swim!

Working on balance, core strength, and overall stability helps improve your body position and shoulder strength in the water. Increasing flexibility will boost your reach and distance per stroke. The more muscular endurance you have, the longer you'll be able to maintain proper technique, and thus the faster you will swim!

Continuous strength gain leads to an increase in propulsion, power, and muscle engagement in the pool. Before I go over a few basic dryland exercises, remember that proper technique is critical. Also, consult a physician before beginning any new routine, and of course be sure to check out the video continent in the supplemental online course for demonstrations of each of these exercises.

Dryland Exercises Without Equipment:

Plank: Strong swimming starts with a strong core! For the plank, place your hands under your shoulders. Try not to hyper-extend your elbows. Creating a straight line from your shoulders to your heels, tuck your pelvis under, and squeeze your butt to maximize core engagement. Think about squeezing your belly button to your spine! You can make this exercise a bit easier by Planking with your knees on the ground, or by placing your hands on an elevated surface.

Squats: Squats will help with general lower body strength for kicking, as well as increasing strength and power for starts and turns. To squat, start with your feet slightly wider than your shoulders. Tuck your pelvis under to remove the arch from your back. Engage your core and drop down into a squat. Engage your glutes and core and drive yourself back up. If you need to make the exercise a bit easier, while improving your technique,, squat to a chair to help with balance.

Pushup: Start in a plank position, with your hands slightly wider than your shoulders. Lower yourself down by bending your elbows, but don't let your shoulders round or shrug! Keep your core and glutes engaged. Pushups will develop your core and upper body strength. To make this exercise easier, pushups can be performed on your knees.

Dead Bug: Lie on your back with your knees bent at a 90° angle and feet off the ground. Extend your hands straight to the ceiling. Extend your right leg and left hand, keeping your opposite arm and leg in the same position. Return to the starting position and repeat on the other side. This can be done with or without a Swiss ball.

Standing ITYW: This exercise strengthens the smaller shoulder muscles that support your rotator cuff. Start by standing tall, then raise your arms forming the letters with your body. I, T, Y, and finally W where your hands are at the same height as your face and you focus on bringing your shoulder blades back to each other.

Superman Extensions: Begin by laying on your stomach with your arms straight out in front of you on the ground. Looking straight down at the floor and keeping your core engaged, lift your arms and legs off the ground. Hold for 1 to 2 seconds and release. This exercise strengthens the small stabilizer muscles in your back to prevent injury!

Hip Bridges: Start lying on your back with your feet planted on the ground. Make sure your lower back is completely flat to the ground. Squeeze your butt and lift up into a bridge position. Hold for 1-2 seconds, making sure your back doesn't arch at the top. Bridges help strengthen the core, glutes, and lower back to prevent injury.

Leg Lifts: Start by laying on your back. With your feet together, point your toes and lift your heels off the ground to a 45° angle to the floor, then lower them to a few centimeters above the ground. To make this easier, place your hands under your bum.

Russian Twists: Sit on the floor, with your torso at a 45° angle. Keeping your back straight, clasp your hands in front of you and rotate side to side. You can keep your heels on the floor for extra stability or float them off the ground. Russian twists develop rotational core strength, which is important for backstroke and freestyle.

Lunge: Stand tall, take a big step back with one leg until your knee almost touches the ground. Then take that same step forward returning both feet together. Repeat with your opposite leg.

Many of the above exercises can be performed with variations that can add complexity and difficulty. Start by mastering the basics, then move to more complicated versions, durations, and add equipment! Below are a series of compound movements that require equipment.

Dryland Exercises With Equipment:

Pullups (Pullup Bar): For a standard grip pullup, grab the pull up bar just wider than shoulder width. Your palms should face away from your body, and your goal should be to pull yourself up from a hanging position so that your chin rises above the level of your hands. The wider apart your hands are, the more difficult this exercise becomes. There are many variations of pull ups, and each version engages your upper body muscles differently. This upper body strength is most applicable to the pulling motion in all the competitive strokes.

Rows (Dumbbells or Bands): Similarly to pullups, rows work the upper body while also developing stability! If you're using resistance bands, drop into a squat position and grip both handles of the band. Pull the handles toward you, keeping your elbows in tight to form a 90° angle. Slowly return to starting position and repeat, holding the squat position for the duration of the interval. This can be performed sitting on a Swiss ball, alternating arms, with dumbbells in a horizontal position, or with a machine.

Squats (Dumbbell, Barbell, Bands): Similarly to when you squat without any resistance, you want to keep a stable body posture. When you squat with weight it's important to pull your bum back and keep your chest up. Focus on keeping your knees behind your toes through the entire range of the squat. I like holding a single dumbbell at my chest level with both of my hands. This is called a "goblet squat" and it's great for developing leg strength and core stability.

Romanian DeadLift (Dumbbell, Barbell, Bands): Use an overhand grip to hold a barbell bar at hip level. Draw your shoulders back and keep your spine straight. Push your hips back as you slowly lower the bar toward your feet. Press your hips forward to come into a standing position with the barbell in front of your thighs. Your knees should be bent slightly. This can be done with Kettlebells as well balancing on a single leg through the movement.

Chest Press (Dumbbell, Barbell, Bands): Similar to a pushup that focuses on engaging your upper body; however, with the chest press, you're on your back and pushing the weight above your body. Lie flat on your back on a bench. Grip the barbell or dumbbells with hands just wider than shoulder-width apart, so when you're at the bottom of the movement of your move your hands are directly above your elbows. Bring the bar slowly down to your chest as you breathe in. Breathe out as you push the bar up. This is also a great exercise to do with resistance bands.

Transferring Strength into the Water

So by now, I hope you're sold that incorporating dryland training into your workout routine is important for a few main reasons. The first being that we know it can prevent injury. This is done by correcting for muscle imbalances in your shoulders and strengthening your core.

Dryland training will also help increase stroke rate by allowing you to take more strokes in less time with more power. This out of water training will also improve distance per stroke by allowing for more power application per stroke. This allows you to swim further with less effort. The goal of any dryland program for swimmers is to become stronger and more explosive in the water while decreasing your risk of injury.

When you swim, focus on maximizing your distance off the

wall in streamline. Take fewer strokes by applying more power per stroke. Think about engaging your core when you swim. Ride high in the water like a hydroplane. When you feel tired, don't let your stroke count fall. Keep your strokes long, and engage your entire body when you swim!

Dryland Training Tips for Beginners

Start with a plan! Don't try and make it up as you go. You're more likely to get hurt and waste your time by just winging it in the gym. In the pool, you can actually get away with this by swimming back and forth without injury. You can't do the equivalent in the gym. Just imagine doing 30 minutes of pushups continuously. This is why I strongly encourage you to check out the workout examples in the supplemental online course and the dryland training programs in the MySwimPro app!

Also, start with a routine that feels manageable. Use your judgment (or consult a personal trainer) to figure out what works for you. If you're struggling on the third rep out of ten, then the weight is too heavy. Alternatively, if you find reps 8–10 of that same set to be challenging with the weight you picked, it's likely the right amount of weight, assuming you have proper technique. As you start to build strength, you can gradually increase your weight load from week to week.

It's also important to make the most of your warm-up time. Taking time to properly warm up is the fitness equivalent to turning your car engine on in the winter a few minutes before you get going! You can maximize your pre-workout time before strength training by doing dynamic stretches.

Finally, avoid working out to exhaustion. This applies both

in and out of the water. You should end your set and workout just before you completely drain your body. You want to finish the workout feeling strong, not like you've just been defeated. That being said, don't be afraid to push it, just be smart and listen to your body!

Let's get after it!

CHAPTER ELEVEN

Injury Prevention

JUST PRIOR TO publishing this book, I challenged myself to swim every single day for 30 days! I wanted to swim over 100,000 meters and raise awareness for men's health issues. I was successful in this journey and actually swam over 120,000 meters by swimming 40 times in 30 days!

I was very proud to complete my 30-day swim challenge, and leading up to this journey of swimming every single day, I was fearful that this increase in training volume and frequency would result in injury. Luckily that was not the case, but I did some strategic planning before starting this challenge to reduce my chances of injury.

Outside of the pool, I did exercises that strengthened the muscles immediately surrounding my shoulders. These stabilizer muscles that keep the rotator cuff healthy need to be focused on and trained just like any other part of our fitness routine.

Holistic swimming means training our body both in and out

of the water. In this chapter, we'll explore how to keep our shoulders and other parts of our body healthy so that we can swim without injury.

Why Do Injuries Happen?

Injuries in swimming are far too common, and for the most part, they're nearly all preventable. Being forced to put your routine on hold is no fun because it takes away from making progress towards something we love. Nearly half of all swimmers report some type of overuse injury.

There are a number of reasons this occurs. Most often, it's poor technique, muscle imbalances, not listening to your body, and having an improper training routine. Combine these factors with a high frequency motion like moving your arm over and over for a freestyle stroke, and it's a disaster waiting to happen.

Just think about how many arm strokes you take in a workout. How about in a week, a month, or a year!? If you take 20 arm strokes per length, swim 5,000 meters per workout 5x/week. That totals 4,000 total arm rotations per day, which is 2,000 rotations for each arm. That's 10,000 rotations per week per arm, and 40,000 rotations per arm per month. In one year, that's nearly half a million arm rotations. One million freestyle strokes! That's insane!

Doing a million of anything is going to cause stress on your body, especially if it's done with resistance. Remember water is 800x more dense than air. This is why swimming with proper technique is so important. You'll repeat the motion millions of times, literally!

Whether you've been exercising for years or are just starting a fitness program, it's important to avoid injuries so you can keep moving closer to your fitness goals. We become more vulnerable to injuries as we get older, in part because we are less agile than we used to be, and we have also lost some of our former bone and muscle mass. We can also lose flexibility as we age.

"Swimmer's Shoulder"

Swimming freestyle or any stroke for that matter requires a highly coordinated, synchronous pattern of muscle firing. USA Swimming ran a survey among its olympic team and found that 66% of Olympic swimmers had a history of shoulder pain and 14% missed a competition due to shoulder pain.

Since our shoulders are the area of our body most likely to be impacted by potential injury we should focus on this area first! Prevention is key, but if you've already experienced pain or discomfort, many of the same principles apply. There are four main causes of the illusive "swimmer's shoulder" that we'll review how to prevent:

1. Muscle fatigue and overload
2. Rotator cuff tendonitis
3. Shoulder laxity
4. Impingement positions during swimming stroke

Prevention

Building off the last chapter on dryland training, it's important to follow a program that develops strength, endurance, muscle balance, and flexibility. These principles are a given for any strength training routine, but focusing on the elements below as they relate to swimming is key.

1. Strengthening the rotator cuff
2. Engaging scapular stabilizers
3. Focusing on the core: Lower back, abs, pelvis
4. Proper stretching:
5. Dynamic stretching before a workout
6. Static stretching after a workout

Below are a series of exercises that focus on developing strength and stability in some of the core areas of the shoulder including the Scapula, Deltoids, Rotator Cuff, and Pelvis. Be sure to check out the supplemental online course for video demonstrations for all of these exercises. The training programs included in the MySwimPro app include all of these exercises in order to have a well-balanced workout experience.

Dryland Exercises for Injury Prevention

Scapula Pushups: Start in a plank position on the knees. Without bending your elbows, lower your body from the shoulder joint. Think about sinking your chest to the floor. Then, press the spot between your shoulder blades to the ceiling, pressing your shoulder blades down and back. This movement strengthens your serratus anterior and improves your scapular mobility to support your shoulder joint and strengthen your pull in all four strokes.

Alphabet: Place a small ball in your palm, and place your palm against a wall. I like using a tennis ball for this one. Extend your arm straight. Begin writing the alphabet letter by letter by rolling the ball on the wall. Repeat with both arms. While it may seem like you're not doing much, you're actually engaging small small stabilizer muscles that support your rotator cuff.

Internal Rotation: Begin lying on your right side, with your knees bent at 90°s. Keep your right arm close to your side and bend it 90°s. Place a weight in your hand. Raise your right hand up toward your left shoulder and lower down. Repeat on the left side. The weight should be minimal. The goal is slow and controlled movements rather than fast powerful swings. These exercises can also be done with a resistance band. The alternative of this movement is the "External rotation," which is the reverse of this movement and strengthens different muscles for stability of the rotator cuff so both are important.

Swiss Ball Alternating Superman: Stabilize your spine to build a strong foundation for all four strokes. Begin with your stomach on a Swiss ball with your hands and feet on the ground. Extend your right arm and left leg, hold for a moment, and return to the starting position. Repeat with the left arm and right leg. You can do this without a ball as well simply on your hands and knees.

Cat Cow Tilts: Start on all fours. Inhale and round your back and tuck your chin, looking down at your belly button. Exhale, arching your back and looking up toward the sky. Repeat, taking deep breaths. This movement strengthens and increases the flexibility of your pelvis, as it actually comes from yoga. This is a great exercise for warming up and cooling down.

Training Modifications if You're Injured

While I'd love to say that the exercises listed above and the routines found in the supplemental online course will undoubt-edly prevent injury, that's simply not true. You can dramatically lower your chances of injury by focusing on improving tech-nique and completing dryland exercises on a regular basis.

Despite all the preventative care you may take, there are certainly instances where injuries will pop up. When they do, it's not the end of the world, and certainly not the end of your swimming journey. If you're injured or simply over-fatigued, there are a few ways you can adapt your workout routine in and out of the water.

Firstly, there are the duration and frequency of your training program. It's okay to take a day (or days) off. Reduce your volume, reduce your frequency, and mix it up. You can change your strokes, remove paddles, and add more kicking sets. You can also try something called vertical kicking where you essen-tially start by treading water and then remove the support of your hands, so that you're only kicking in a vertical body position.

With vertical kicking, you can do flutter kick, dolphin kick, or breaststroke kick. This can be done with your hands at the surface level of the water, or with your arms above the water in streamline and everywhere in between. I like mixing in vertical kicking sets even if I'm not injured just to mix up training and focus on developing my kick strength.

Additionally, you can swim with fins. These allow you to increase propulsion and decrease the load on your shoulders. For some swimmers adding a pull buoy can have the same effect. If you have a lower body injury, focusing on pulling with a pull buoy or just completely shutting off your legs will help alleviate some of the stress caused by swimming.

Outside of the water, make sure you're doing a dynamic

warmup to activate your muscles and get your heart rate elevated. This will get the blood flowing and improve circulation before getting in the water. If you're injured, stop dryland training or swimming that causes pain. Additionally, stop other non-swimming activities that cause pain or fatigue muscles that you know will be needed for swimming.

When it comes to technique, focus on balancing your stroke cycle. If you're used to breathing only on one side, mix it up with bilateral breathing and focus on balancing your technique. Rotate evenly to both sides and try not to cross the midline with your hand entry or pull. Increase your body roll to maximize your distance per stroke and use rotational momentum to decrease stress on your shoulders.

Recovery

One of the major benefits of swimming for fitness is that it's low impact on your body. Unlike running or other land-based physical activity, swimming doesn't put as much wear and tear on your joints and muscles (particularly your knees). Even though swimming may not cause the same aches and pains of these other sports, it's still important that you give yourself an opportunity to recover after intense training or swimming competitions.

Our body needs rest days (or at least recovery workouts) to perform at our highest level and maximize the time we spend in the water. It's important to know a couple of things about recovery and rest in general:

Can you swim everyday? How long should you rest?

During strenuous exercise such as resistance training or aerobic threshold intervals, muscle tissue develops micro-tears in response to stress. Immediately following exercise, the recovery process begins through acute inflammation.

An "active recovery" swim workout could be added or in place of higher intensity swim workouts in a weekly routine. For example, swimming lower volume at lower intensities will allow the body to stay active, circulate blood and maintain a feel for the water without furthering the body's level of fatigue.

I personally like to swim every other day, alternating out of water dryland training. Swimming is a great way to maintain the feel of the water while serving as active recovery for my lifting session out of the water. When I need to ramp up my training volume in the pool, I'll keep track of how much intensity vs. volume I do per workout and per week to make sure I'm not burning myself out.

Dynamic Stretching vs. Static Stretching

Whether you swim every day or once per week, experts agree that a dynamic warm-up prepares your body best for peak output and reduces your chances of injury. Static stretching, on the other hand, can actually impair performance and negatively impact shoulder stability if done before a swim workout.

To clarify the differences between these two, just know that dynamic stretching improves flexibility and range of motion, just like static stretching does. However, when done before a workout, dynamic stretching can boost your power and strength.

Dynamic stretching would be performing movements like arm swings, arm circles, butt kicks, and dynamic hamstring stretch. Basically, movements that stretch the muscle, but only for a short period of time. You don't want to hold the stretch before performing the workout. On the flip side, a static stretch, is where you actually hold the position and perform several cycles of breathing while in the position.

This could be reaching to touch your toes stretching the back of your legs, or holding your arm parallel across your body to stretch your shoulder. Be sure to check out the supplemental online course for full dryland warmups and cool downs that can be done before and after workouts.

It's important to remember that many injuries in swimming are due to overuse and improper technique. The primary prevention strategy should be establishing improving technique, establishing strength, muscle endurance, and flexibility. Having a well balanced dryland routine will help increase your odds of staying healthy so you can swim longer and continue to improve!

Finally, always consult a physician if symptoms persist.

CHAPTER TWELVE

Nutrition

HAVE you ever heard the expression, "you are what you eat"?

Does this mean if you eat a lot of carrots, you'll turn orange? No, but on a figurative level, you are in fact what you eat. I mean, think about it. Over the course of a day, you might eat three to five times. Over the course of just one year, that's thousands of meals you will have eaten. Just think about all that food!

Therefore, what you fuel your body with is critical to not only your performance but also your overall health in and out of the water. Whether your goal is to lose weight, gain muscle, or simply feel better, having the right understanding of what to eat, when, and why can dramatically improve your likelihood of success!

Nutrition for Swimmers

Diet affects performance at every level, and the foods that

we choose in training and competition will affect how well we perform in workouts. Even beyond our workouts, our diet impacts how we feel, think and act at all hours of the day. Our diet even impacts our sleep routine which is huge to our recovery and feeling refreshed for the next day.

You need to be aware of your nutritional goals and of how to create an eating strategy that meets those goals. Diet may have its biggest impact during training, and a good diet will help support consistent intensive training while reducing the risk of illness or injury.

Good food choices can also optimize the adaptations in muscle and other tissues in response to the training stimulus. Everyone is different, and there is no single diet that meets the needs of all people at all times. Your needs as a human will change during the week, month, and year, so it's important to be flexible to accommodate this. Getting the right amount of energy to stay healthy and to tolerate the changes in a workout routine is a key goal in managing a balanced diet.

Consume too much and body fat increases: too little and performance falls and illness results. Developing your ideal physique requires careful integration of training and diet. Carbohydrates are a key nutrient for energy supply, but the amount of carbohydrates depends on the training load and therefore varies from day to day.

Protein is important and necessary for building and repairing muscles, but a varied diet containing everyday foods will generally supply more than enough protein. The timing and type of protein is as important as the amount of protein in the diet. If you're vegetarian, this is not a problem, as you can still meet all your protein needs.

A nutrient-rich diet that meets energy needs and is based

largely on vegetables, fruits, beans, legumes, grains, lean animal meats, dairy produce and oils should also ensure an adequate intake of vitamins and minerals. Additionally, maintaining hydration is important for performance. An adequate intake of fluid before, during, and after a workout is critical.

Food is an important part of our lives, and you should enjoy the foods that you eat. In this chapter we're going to overview how to fuel your body before, during, and after workouts. We'll also explore some different ways to stay field and hydrated during all-day events like competitions, and longer endurance swims.

The Nutrition Equation

Similar to the swimming equation, there's an equation for nutrition, and it's actually even simpler! The equation states that our energy balance is equal to the amount of energy we take in minus the amount of energy we expend.

Energy Balance = Energy Intake – Energy Expenditure

Simply put, calories in minus calories out must be equal. If you're trying to lose weight, you must expend more calories than you're intaking. This is an overly simplified model, but it's used to keep things in perspective and really make you realize that you ultimately have a lot of control over your body weight and energy output.

We can further this concept with regard to your energy in a singular workout. All we have to do is break it down to the amount of energy you will input to your body minus the total energy expenditure during the exercise minus the background cost of being sedentary during this period. In other words, you're still burning calories even when you're not swimming and just standing at the wall between sets.

Energy Availability = Energy Intake – Energy Cost of Training (or Competition)

Remember, swimming is a very demanding activity. Your body is moving through a medium that's 800x more resistive than air. This resistance causes a high level of energy expenditure just to move forward. Your entire body is engaged, your heart rate rises, and you expend energy, aka burning calories!

So, how many calories do you burn while swimming?

The rate at which your body burns calories for energy is known as your metabolism. When you exercise, this rate increases. Just how much and for how long depends on a wide variety of factors including: gender, body composition, and most importantly your level of exertion.

First, your weight plays a big role in how much you burn. Generally, the more you weigh, the more you burn. Additionally, your metabolism is also an important factor in how many calories are burned. In one hour of swimming, a 130-pound person swimming freestyle will burn 590 calories swimming fast, and 413 calories swimming slower. A 205-pound person on the other hand swimming freestyle for one hour will burn 931 calories swimming fast, and 651 calories swimming slower.

Freestyle is the most efficient stroke, and therefore burns the least calories all things considered. Even though you'll burn fewer calories at a relaxed pace, swimming freestyle is the most sustainable stroke. Butterfly, on the other hand, may burn up to twice as many calories per unit of time, but you won't be able to swim butterfly for extended periods of time.

. . .

What to Eat Before, During, After Swimming?

If you are what you eat, it's important you eat the right foods before, during, and after swimming or your dryland workout. Below is a list of recommended foods chosen not only for their nutritional value but also for how your body feels after eating them.

NOTE: Always consult a nutritionist for specific and personalized dietary recommendations. This is particularly important if you have any dietary restrictions or allergies, e.g. Celiac's.

Before Swimming

Ideally, a meal should be eaten 3-4 hours before a workout or competition. It should provide 1.5 grams per pound of body weight of carbohydrates. Adding small amounts of protein can aid in regulating energy levels by slowing down the absorption of carbohydrates. So, what does this mean in terms of real food?

Some meal ideas 3-4 hours before a workout or event include spaghetti with meat sauce, pasta with chicken and vegetables, and grilled chicken with rice. A turkey or tuna sandwich is also a good source of carbs and protein. For snacks, think about adding an oatmeal raisin walnut granola bar, trail mix with nuts or raisins, or a single serving of fruit juice.

If you're eating 2-3 hours before a workout, consider eating a baked potato, bagel with peanut butter, fruit smoothie, or oatmeal. You can also try nonfat yogurt, pancakes, or fresh fruit. As you get closer to the workout, you'll need to reduce the overall amount of both carbohydrates and protein you consume.

If you have one hour or less before your swim workout, you'll want to eat something light. Some great examples of this include raisins, a banana, a ½ bagel, a fig bar, or applesauce. Toast, crackers, and pretzels can be great, just be sure to watch your portion size.

Additionally, you can consume a sports drink, but be sure that this drink contains electrolytes and carbohydrates, and not caffeine or other stimulants. It's important that you're hydrated at all hours of the day. If you feel thirsty before you even start a workout, it most likely means you're dehydrated so it's important to continuously monitor fluid intake.

During Swimming

If your workout lasts longer than 60 minutes, it's important to consume some carbohydrates. This can be done through a sports drink or gel and ensures that your muscles receive adequate amounts of energy, especially during the later stages of a competition or a workout.

Consume 6-12 ounces of a sports drink with 6-8% carbohydrates every 15-30 minutes during your swim workout. Just for reference, one gulp is about two ounces, so about three to six gulps every half hour. Your sports drink needs to contain enough water to avoid cramps.

For high intensity activities, sports drinks and gels containing multiple forms of sugar can increase absorption and delivery of carbohydrates. If you're swimming less than 60 minutes, simply drinking water will be more than enough to keep you hydrated.

It's important to note that sports drinks should not be confused with "energy drinks," which typically contain stimulants. Additionally their carbohydrate concentration is normally greater than 10%. Sports drinks are beverages that contain electrolytes and carbohydrates, not caffeine and other stimulants, for example Gatorade or Powerade.

After Swimming

It's key to eat a carbohydrate snack within 30 minutes after a swim workout to allow the body to start replenishing glycogen stores in the body. Even if you can't eat a full meal immediately after the swim, it's important to at least have 0.65 grams of carbohydrates per pound of body weight within the first 30 minutes after exercise.

I always recommend a banana and bagel if you can bring that with you. The average banana has 31 grams of carbs, and a bagel has 52 grams of carbs. This "post workout snack" should be followed by an additional "full meal" within two hours of completing the swim workout. It's important to consume a couple of meals high in carbohydrates within six hours after swimming to ensure that the muscles continue the glycogen restoration.

In terms of hydration, drink three cups of fluid for each pound lost during the workout. In the water, it's hard to tell how much "water weight" you've lost. A common myth is that swimmers do not sweat in the water. This is false, and swimmers do sweat in the pool. It's important to hydrate yourself before, during, and after a workout!

Hydration

Hydration is one of the most important nutritional components for a swimmer of any level. Over 60% of your body is water and as you train, fluid is lost through your skin through sweat and through the lungs while breathing. If this fluid is not replaced at regular intervals during a workout, it will lead to dehydration.

If you become dehydrated, you will have a decreased volume of blood circulating through your body and consequently the amount of blood pumped with each heartbeat decreases. Additionally, the muscles that you're engaging will not receive enough oxygen. As a result, exhaustion sets in, and your performance will suffer.

The best way to prevent dehydration is to maintain your body's fluid levels by consuming floods before, during, and after your swim workout. You can monitor your fluid loss in two ways. The first is simply weighing yourself before and after a workout. Remember, for every pound lost during the workout, drink three cups of fluids to rehydrate your body.

Another way you can monitor your hydration level is by monitoring the color of your urine. Urine that is dark gold indicates dehydration. If your urine is pale lemonade or weak tea color, it's a sign that you're hydrated.

Most people don't feel thirsty until more than 2 percent of your body weight is lost. By this point, it's too late, and you've already become dehydrated. For best results, keep a bottle of fluid available with you and drink every 15-20 minutes while you workout!

Supplements

If you're looking for a competitive edge or something just to help you reach your fitness goals, supplements may be something to consider. However, there are no quick-fix supplements for improving sports performance. Consuming a wide variety of foods and staying well hydrated are the basic ingredients to reaching peak performance.

If you're competing and subject to drug testing, you must tread carefully because dietary supplements may cause a positive test for a prohibited substance that may not be disclosed on the product label. Some dietary supplements include vitamins, minerals, amino acids, herbs, and other organic tissues and metabolites.

While some mainstream supplements are made by responsible manufacturers, a growing number of supplement products contain dangerous and undisclosed ingredients like steroids, stimulants, and other drugs. Rather than relying on advertisements from companies who are trying to sell you their product, you as a consumer have the responsibility to educate yourself on what you're putting into your body.

While there is no such thing as a magic diet or food, there are many ways in which eating well will allow you to achieve your specific goals. It makes no sense to train hard and ignore the benefits that good food choices offer to maximize training and performance. Remember, you are what you eat!

CHAPTER THIRTEEN

Mental Training

I'D LIKE you to think about the last time you tried a new hobby, sport, or fitness-related skill. Maybe it was learning how to ski, or think about the very first time you learned a new technique in the pool. Was it easy? Did you struggle at it?

Did that struggle give you a boost of motivation, or did it make you feel hopeless?

If you respond to these challenges in life with a renewed sense of motivation, you most likely have a growth mindset. If you feel helpless and discouraged, you probably fall in with the majority of people who have more of a fixed mindset.

The good news is that you can actually change this limiting mindset. And when you do, you'll open up a whole new world of possibilities and make more progress on your swimming journey than you ever before thought possible!

Growth vs. Fixed Mindset

With a fixed mindset, you generally believe that your skills and abilities are predetermined. Think about something as basic as learning how to swim. We all learned this skill at one point. The earlier in our life we learned this skill, the less we remember it. If you learn how to swim as an adult, your preconceived notions and fears around the water are significant inhibitors to just getting started.

This is the same concept for any skill in swimming. A few examples of these "skills" include learning how to do a flip turn, bilateral breathing, underwater dolphin kicking, and many, many more. If you have a fixed mindset, you might think that there is no hope to learn these new skills because you're either good at it or you're not. People with this mindset tend to believe that there's not much you can do to change this.

With a growth mindset, you believe that no matter where you're starting from, you can improve. If you have a growth mindset around swimming, you believe you can improve your technique, become more efficient, and swim faster, no matter where you're starting from.

People with a growth mindset excel in all facets of life, not just in fitness and swimming. It's an important concept to discuss and understand because by doing so, you will be able to unlock an incredible amount of potential within yourself.

Hard work, proper goal setting, and perseverance will get you to where you want to be, but you have to first start by believing that you can get there regardless of where you are now. If you have a fixed mindset around your swimming performance, then your underlying belief is that no matter what you do, you won't improve.

It's important to note that having a growth vs. fixed mindset isn't always black and white. For example, if you learned how to swim as a child, you have probably always found that floating or treading water relatively easy. You're probably confident that if you want to get better at treading water, floating, or even swimming, that if provided with clear goals, a good plan, and the right support system you'll be able to improve these skills relatively quickly.

Yet, when it comes to running, you might believe you're just terrible at it. You may have been told that swimmers are not good at running and vice versa. So if you're good at running, you can't be good at swimming and if you're a fish in the water, you're not going to be athletic on land.

If you truly believe that you'll never get better at something, you're unlikely to put any necessary time or effort required to actually make progress. It's a toxic mindset that only holds you back. If you don't put in the effort, you're not going to improve. It's pretty simple. This is why mindset is so critical. Regardless of where you fall on the mindset spectrum right now, you can change it!

Developing a Growth Mindset

I truly believe that no matter where you're starting from, you can improve. Yes, it will be hard work, and it will take time, but it will always be worth it when you look back at how far you've come.

Having a growth mindset is the first step in the process, but it won't get you very far if you don't do any actual work. To really see measurable progress, you have to work on setting both short- and long-term goals, then break them down into achievable milestones. In the next section, we'll go into detail on how to set SMART goals for yourself to be successful.

If you want to make progress towards a big long-term goal like losing weight, qualifying for a competition, or even breaking a world record, you not only have to believe you can get better, you also need to place effort before talent. For example, it's easy to look at a swim team practice and see that a few of the kids naturally seem to swim faster than the rest of the group.

Are these swimmers more coordinated or more physically developed? Why are they moving faster than the other swimmers? What you can't see from this snapshot alone is what will happen with the slower swimmers if they work harder than their more talented-seeming peers, Most of these swimmers will actually surpass the other kids at some point. You must believe that effort is more important than initial talent to have a growth mindset.

Another key mindset shift is learning to develop the skill of perseverance. Some call it grit, toughness, or downright hustle. Developing grit means combining persistence, ambition, and self-discipline to chase big goals that might take months, years, or even decades to accomplish.

This tenacity is what allows you to stick with your goals when you reach snags and roadblocks along the way. We all experience failure in some way or another, and that's okay. It's going to happen!

> I can accept failure, everyone fails at something, but I can't accept not trying. – Michael Jordan

Failure is something we all experience at some point. It's nothing to be ashamed of; if anything it should be embraced. Whether it's missing the wall on a flip turn, getting disqualified in your best event or flunking an exam at school, it is something that we all experience, and it's totally normal and actually healthy.

Sometimes failure is a reality check to keep us humble and motivated. Other times, failure just down right sucks. Regardless of how you fail, or what you fail in, what's most important is what you do next!

Having a growth mindset is incredibly vulnerable because when you give yourself a shot to try something you care about, you're also setting yourself up for a potential failure. If you don't allow yourself to fail, you won't allow yourself to really try.

The more challenging the goal, the harder you'll have to work for it. It doesn't matter if your goal is to drop 1 second in your 50m freestyle time or qualify for the Olympic team, it all starts with a growth mindset.

· · ·

Mental Training

So, how do you develop and train a growth mindset?

Mental factors such as confidence, composure, focus, and motivation are highly significant to improving your chances of success. In athletics, there's an entire industry of sports psychology professionals that are focused on optimizing an athlete's mental training to reach peak performance.

This is not just about maximizing athletic output but also minimizing the psychological effects of poor performance. Psychology principles such as positive thinking, imagery, and goal setting can be applied to swimming goals to help you perform and prepare for an individual workout, a season, and your entire swimming career. At the elite levels, all swimmers have the talent and the physical tools to compete at an incredibly high level. What separates these athletes is what happens between the ears. It's mental training.

Mental training is the segment of sports psychology that concentrates specifically on breaking through the mental barriers that are keeping you from performing at peak potential. Remember, this concept extends beyond just swimming and makes its way into our daily life. Having a growth mindset paired with the right mental training allows us to theoretically achieve whatever we set our minds to.

> You can't put a limit on anything. The more you dream, the farther you get. - Michael Phelps

It's easier to embrace mental training when you fully under-stand it and its benefits. However, the best way to embrace mental training is when you actually experience its power first-hand. Mental training is about improving your attitude and mental skills to help perform at your best by identifying limiting beliefs and embracing a healthier philosophy about the sport.

Mental skills, just like any physical skill, take repetition, practice, and real-time application to develop! This means working on your mental fitness on a daily basis. It also means identifying any mental barriers that are holding you back. Mental barriers include perfectionism, the fear of failure, and a lack of emotional control.

When I was in high school, our swim coach ran us through a visualization activity in the weeks leading up to our conference championships meet. Every day before we got in the water to start the swim portion of our workout, we laid down on our towels and closed our eyes. Our coach asked us to simply relax and visualize the "big day".

He used vivid language to describe the atmosphere of the swimming competition, the aroma of chlorine on the pool deck, and of course the sights and sounds of the swimming venue. He spoke in great detail allowing us to formulate a mental model of our ideal race. From how we were called onto the starting block, then diving in, approaching the first turn, and finally, touching the wall and seeing the scoreboard with our goal time.

Visualization is a very powerful skill, and similarly to any physical skill, it takes time to develop. Mental training is an incredible skill to have in your tool kit. Remember, the mind controls the body and the mind is unlimited!

Your Mind is a Muscle — Let's Flex It.

If you want to get physically stronger, you'll need to work-out. This is pretty simple and obvious for our physical attributes, but it also holds true for our mental strength. Through training, we can change our brains to become even more mentally strong, healthier, and fitter.

Think of your mind as a muscle. When I talk about our mind's strength, I'm referring to different mental abilities we can access, strengthen, and flex. This mental strength supports us in feeling creative, resilient, happy, and successful.

We don't get strong arms by doing bicep curls only once. Our mental strength is the same. Improving our mental muscles' performance requires time, practice, and consistency. This can be done through a number of ways, including visualization, which was already mentioned, but also in ways that do not directly relate to swimming.

Training your mind's muscle is a lifestyle priority. Oftentimes, this mental fitness doesn't actually take that long to develop on a daily basis, you just need to be consistent. It could be as simple as 10 minutes of morning meditation, prioritizing sleep, prayer, taking time to reflect everyday, or connecting with a loved one.

If you notice that some of these activities are overwhelming or trigger feelings of anxiety, then I recommend reaching out and getting support from a trusted friend, a therapist, or a health-care practitioner. While it's helpful to be independent and self-sufficient in some areas of life, it's wise to seek support where you may need help. One of the greatest acts of courage and developing mental strength is taking the initiative to ask for help.

Slowing down and deepening your breath can help calm the mind. It can also reduce blood pressure, improve memory, and settle emotions. Meditation is a great way to practice concentration, equanimity, clarity, and friendliness with yourself.

Take a moment and reflect, how would you describe yourself when you are feeling mentally strong, healthy, and fit?

Taking Action

Are you excited by the prospect of swimming?

Are you excited to jump in the water tomorrow? or today? — or would you rather not think about it at all?

Try writing down your feelings about swimming in a quick, five-minute, stream-of-consciousness burst. This can help indicate your current train of thought. It's perfectly normal to want to put these thoughts off to the side or just not think about it. Ordinarily, I would agree with you, but since you're reading a book on how to improve your swimming, I'll challenge you anyway!

At some point, you'll need to specify your intentions, write SMART goals, and take action. Many people aim too high, setting unrealistic expectations (I'm going to swim twice a day every single day!) and unattainable goals (I'm going to break the world record next month!). But this approach seldom works, and it can lead to feelings of failure and hopelessness.

In the next section, we'll dive into how to set SMART goals so you can be successful! This all starts with a growth mindset and holistic approach to training that includes both your physical regimen and also your mental training. We'll dig into why you swim and how to get started!

COOL DOWN:

Swim for life

CHAPTER FOURTEEN

Why We Swim

SWIMMING IS TRULY a one of a kind experience, and nothing else will engage all your senses like the feeling of being in the water. There's something about the feeling of weightlessness that is special, and it is this feeling that is one of the many joys the sport of swimming offers humanity.

There's a euphoric feeling of being in the water that's unique. When we find comfort in this magical medium called water, we feel at home. There are many reasons to swim, and too many to list here, but it's important for yourself to understand WHY you swim. When you understand your "why," you'll be able to better position yourself for success regardless of what your goals are.

The Golden Circle

If someone asked you how you stay fit, you'd likely reply something along the lines of "I swim", I go to the gym", "I lift weights", or "I don't really workout". All of these responses are perfectly valid, but they don't really spark any emotion.

It's very easy to understand "what" you do to stay in shape and even "how" you do it, but it's often hard to uncover "why" we do what we do. It's important to dig deeper into this topic because once we understand the underlying emotion and drivers of our actions, we are better able to impact them and achieve a desired outcome.

A famous thought leader and author named Simon Sinek popularized a concept of a Golden Circle. The model he developed is an attempt to explain why some people and organizations are particularly able to inspire others and differentiate themselves successfully. These concepts can easily be applied to our life goals and swimming ambitions specifically. The neuroscience behind the Golden Circle theory is that humans respond best when messages communicate with those parts of the brain that control emotions, behavior, and decision making.

At the outer core, we think about "what" we do. For the scope of our golden circle analogy, we'll focus on swimming. We'll reference two individuals. A young man named John who swims three times per week and an older woman named Susan who goes swimming in the ocean every morning. When we move from the outer core towards the middle of the Golden Circle, we enter the next layer: "How." Now the discussion is not about what you do, but how you do it.

For example, John who swims three times per week does so by following a specific training plan in the MySwimPro app. Susan on the other hand goes open water swimming every morning by meeting a group of friends at 6AM by Tower 30 and swimming parallel to the shoreline for 2 km. As you can see with each layer of the golden circle, we get more specific and really start to understand how John and Susan build a swimming routine.

Most people stop there. They go only two layers deep. At the core of the Golden Circle is Why. We need to understand why we do what we do. Why does John swim three times per week and Susan swim in the ocean every morning?

John swims three times per week because his goal is to lose 5 kilograms before his wedding date. He used to be a runner, but due to injuring his knee, and several operations later, he's no longer able to run for cardio. John used to swim on a team growing up, so he picked it back up to increase his cardio before his wedding date.

Susan, on the other hand, swims in the ocean every morning because she's been doing this same routine for the last 30 years. Her morning swim group has become her family. What started as a fun way to kickoff the day with friends has become a ritual and meditative escape from the stresses of the world.

Both John and Susan recognize the incredible health benefits of swimming, yet their "why" is completely different. John is motivated by results and has a specific numeric goal he's working towards. Susan uses swimming as a mental break from the world and a way to structure her day and her life. John and Susan both swim, but their how and why are very different. It's important to dig into why you do what you do.

Why do *you* swim?

There really is no right or wrong answer to this question, but it's important to take a moment and reflect on why you do what you do. If you can find where your internal drive comes from, and then associate your goals to this intrinsic motivation, you'll be much more successful in reaching your dreams! You'll also enjoy the journey of swimming that much more!

Why Swim?

There are many reasons to swim!

Physical fitness is a given, but there's so much more than just being fit and having a certain physique. Of course, there's the mental health element of swimming which is huge. It's pretty remarkable to be in an environment where you can escape from the world. Add in the zero gravity effect of water, and it's as if you've teleported to outer space!

Many swim because they've found routine in the daily dip before or after the work day. Adding structure to your day or week can make you more productive in all areas of your life. I personally know many people who swim because it's all they know, and they're perfectly fine sticking with it! They feel no need to pick up another form of fitness. Swimming works for them, and they have no intention to change it.

On the flip side, there are many people who swim because

they can no longer do another form of fitness due to injury or other restrictions, and now they rely on the water. Swimming is also great for cross training and rehabilitation from injury. Many top athletes from other sports use the pool to add an element of resistance training that can't be done on land.

For others, swimming is a competitive pursuit. It's all about being the best version of yourself in the water, optimizing your technique and training to reach a specific, measurable goal. Qualifying for a meet or performing a best time in a specific event becomes the core focus of your swimming. For me, I sometimes fall into this category when I have something specific to train for. I love preparing for a pool competition or open water race that allows me to focus my training and push my body to its limits.

A segment of this competitive group also loves adventure. The world is filled with beauty, and many swimmers take advantage of unique events and open water races all over the planet to explore the world. Later in this book, I outline some of these experiences including the opportunity to swim from Asia to Europe in the Bosphorus Cross Continental swim. It's an incredible experience and there are many venture seekers who simply swim to continue participating in these incredible events.

I have many friends who love the camaraderie of swimming in a group workout setting. They prefer going to a pool that's filled with people. Saying hello to the lifeguards, pool staff, and if they swim on a team, enjoying the social element of the sport. Certainly swimming can be a solitary activity, but there are opportunities to enjoy each other's company before the workout gets started, between sets, and after a workout. It's also fantastic to have other swimmers to push you to be your best in the middle of difficult training sessions.

Finally, there's an element of intrigue about swimming that's hard to put my finger on. It's truly a unique experience that's unlike anything else. Take an opportunity and really think about why you swim. Why do you do what you do? Understanding why you swim will help you structure your goals, training plan, and time in the water to enjoy the sport to its full potential!

CHAPTER FIFTEEN

How To Get Started

IN THIS CHAPTER, I'm going to share a simple process for how you can turn your why into a specific action plan to reach your goals. This might be the most important chapter you'll ever read if you have not gotten started yet OR if you have never set SMART goals before. I'll break down exactly what SMART goals are, how to to write them, and how to get started.

If you have not already done so, please checkout the supplemental online course for exclusive video content and document templates that matchup with each chapter of this book. Also, be sure to join the MySwimPro global community facebook group. This is 100% free and accessible to swimmers who have purchased this book. This group and all other digital resources will be linked in the supplemental online course.

SMART Goals

Swimmers in general are very ambitious people, but oftentimes, we'll bite off more than we can chew. A resolution without a plan is just wishful thinking, so it's super important to set SMART Goals for yourself.

If you want long-term success, be clear about what you want to accomplish. Recall your why. When setting goals, it's crucial that they be very defined and methodical in your approach. To help you succeed, use the S.M.A.R.T. goal process. SMART is an acronym for the five building blocks necessary to reach any goal.

S – Specific
M – Measurable
A – Achievable
R – Relevant
T – Time-Bound

Make sure your goals are specific and stated in performance terms. For instance, if you want to drop time, your goal might be "to drop 2.00 seconds in the 200 meter freestyle at the regional championships in 12 weeks." If you want to improve your flip turn, your goal might be "to swim 500 meters continuously with flip turns at every turn by the end of the year."

A goal is measurable when it is easy to determine if it was accomplished. In swimming, dropping time is easily measured. In the prior example, 12 weeks from now you will either drop 2 seconds or not in the 200 meter freestyle. Likewise, for the flip turn goal, it will be easy to determine if you are successful in accomplishing that goal because there was a metric associated to it: swim 500 meters with a flip turn at every turn.

Conversely, a goal to "swim faster" is not very measurable. A better goal is to swim a specific distance in a specific period of time. Your goal does not have to be doing a best time to be measurable. Maybe your goal is to lose weight. Great, how much weight? Perhaps your goal is more technique oriented and you'd like to swim more efficiently. A great goal for efficiency is swimming with an average distance per stroke, stroke count, or SWOLF. The key is to add a metric so you can measure your progress towards a specific goal.

One of the biggest mistakes people make while setting goals is that they set something unattainable. Goals should be set high, but they must also be realistic. A goal to drop 20 seconds in four weeks in the 100 meter freestyle is both unrealistic and unhealthy. Likewise, if you are new to swimming and you set a goal to finish a 5k open water swim in one month, you're setting yourself up for failure, pain, and disappointment. Make your goals challenging but also attainable.

Additionally, your goals should be important to you. They must be relevant! Don't follow a goal just because your friends, family members, or teammates have set that goal on your behalf. Your goals are your motivators to continue exercising, so make sure they are important to you. Remember why you swim, and set your goals accordingly.

Make sure each goal has a specific time frame for completion. SMART goals need to be Time-bound. This allows you to easily determine if the goal has been achieved on a specific date. It also increases the likelihood that you will accomplish each goal since you know the clock is ticking. For example, the goal "to drop 2.00 seconds at the regional championships in 12 weeks" has a time frame.

Whether it's 12 weeks from your start date or on a specific

day, it's important to set a goal with a timeline in the next few months. Any longer than this, and it becomes a macro goal which you'll need several micro goals or "checkpoints" along the way to keep you on track. I advise having both yearly goals and quarterly goals to keep yourself accountable in the short run while you work your way to the year-end or seasonal goal.

Avoid fluffy goals at all costs! A fluffy goal is something that does not meet any of the criteria listed in the SMART goal methodology. This would be saying something like: I want to swim faster. That's not a goal, it's a wish. Unfortunately, wishful thinking doesn't make goals happen.

> "A dream without a goal is a wish. A goal without a plan is just a dream." - Antoine de Saint-Exupéry

Another common fluffy goal I see over and over is the notion around losing weight. "I want to lose weight" is not a goal. It's great to have the initial drive to make that statement, but you can't stop there. Let's put together a plan and re-write that wish so it becomes a SMART Goal.

A SMART Goal for weight loss might be something like: "My goal is to lose 10 kilograms by July 31st. I will do this by swimming three times per week for 30-45 minutes following the weight loss swim plan in the MySwimPro app. I will meal prep twice per week and weight myself once per week and check in with my best friend who is also following the same weight loss program."

This goal is brilliant. It's specific, measurable, attainable, and time-bound. It's also relevant to the goal of the swimmer, and it is routed with intrinsic motivation. This is key and would be further amplified by understanding why this individual is trying to lose weight. Remember the Golden Circle: it's easy to understand the outer shell, but if we can dig deeper into the underlying motivations, we can be significantly more successful in achieving our goals.

Make SMARTER Goals

SMART is a fantastic acronym, but there's something missing from this formula. A more complete formula adds an important final step: "Re-Evaluate". A SMARTER goal means there's a feedback loop to re-evaluate and redo the goal as needed. Goals can change, so establish clarity around success and failure. The final thing to remember when it comes to achieving large goals is to actually jump in and get started.

This is why breaking your goals into rituals and process goals is so important. As human beings, we're wired to avoid disappointment. If your goals feel unachievable, you'll start to self sabotage. Don't work against your brain. Embrace these limitations and work with smaller, more manageable goals and rituals.

You can turn simple behaviors into rituals with process goals. Process goals focus on the implementation of your swimming program. For example, a good process goal is swimming four times per week for 60 minutes. On the flip side, thinking that you're going to go swimming whenever you can or whenever you feel like it just won't cut it. You have more control over accomplishing a goal when there is a set schedule around it. This will also help you get in the habit of swimming with a regular routine to achieve your goal.

Other process goals as they relate to swimming could include:

- Take at least three dolphin kicks off every wall in every workout
- Log and keep track of all your workouts in the MySwimPro app
- Complete two dryland sessions per week in addition to swimming
- Breaststroke pullout past 10m off every wall
- No breathing off of a flip turn
- Swim an additional 200 meters of breaststroke after every swim

It's also important to determine roadblocks that may keep you from reaching your goals and make a plan to get around them. Don't chase other people's goals; set your own goals for yourself. Make sure you're passionate about your own goal. Write out your SMART goals. Yes, with a sheet of paper and a pen. Get it documented and all the steps you need to get there, to hold yourself accountable. Anticipate set-backs but don't get discouraged if you get off track. Instead, focus on the end goal.

Finally, don't set goals that someone else has power over. Make sure all your goals are at your own control. No one can control your outcome. This puts you in a position of both power and self-accountability. Also, be sure to approach writing SMARTER goals with a positive attitude. Remember, you want to be ambitious but also realistic. The mind controls the body and the mind is unlimited!

Finding a Personalized Plan

Understanding your why will help you choose a specific goal and stick with it. To reach your full potential and optimize your time, you'll need the right plan to help you get there. The hardest part is making a commitment to following a plan and actually getting started. Once you do get started, then what?

"The secret of getting ahead is getting started." – Mark Twain

Following a structured plan that is aligned with your goals is the best way to succeed! Properly designed training plans help you progress safely, avoiding injury, and building long-term results. In the online supplemental course, I share a swim workout template and also how to construct a training plan from scratch.

The MySwimPro App

I started MySwimPro to help swimmers improve their performance and health. The app essentially works as a personal swim coach wherever and whenever you need them. By dynamically adapting workouts and training programs, it offers a personal workout experience as if you had a personal swim coach guiding you through workouts set by set.

Over the years, the platform has developed to include various wearable integrations, analytics, video content, and more. We continue to evolve the platform and deliver an even more personalized training experience for swimmers around the world regardless of skill level. In the online supplemental course, I share more about the app, how to use it, and an exclusive discount to our premium subscription membership.

Additionally, be sure to join the MySwimPro global community Facebook group. You'll join tens of thousands of swimmers from all over the world, from beginner to pro, who are all passionate about swimming faster and smarter than ever before. So whether you're a beginner swimmer or elite athlete, you've come to the right place!

Having a support network is huge to not only keep you accountable but also inspire you to do your best and reach for your dreams. You can connect with me in that group, and a few other resources I'll list in the online supplemental course. Wishing you the very best in your journey, and happy swimming :)!

CHAPTER SIXTEEN

My Gold Medal Moments

I BELIEVE that we are all just one step away from achieving our Gold Medal Moment. We just need the right guidance, structure, and support to make it happen.

At the start of the book, I shared my five promises and the intentions behind them. The first promise was to share a fresh perspective with you on swimming in general. How I can present thought-provoking information that will make you think critically about your swimming. I also wanted to inform you through a technical breakdown of each stroke and how to swim faster with a holistic approach.

One of the promises was to help you learn how to set SMART goals, remembering that a dream without a goal is a wish, and a goal without a plan is just a dream. We all have our own unique motivations to swim and you might be curious to learn a bit more about myself and my swimming journey. What are some of my greatest passions around the water?

That brings us to my final promise of the book, to inspire you! You don't have to win gold to achieve something great!

In this last chapter, I'll share five personal stories from my swimming story. In the supplemental videos online, you can watch me do video interviews with incredible human beings. You will hear from people just like yourself who are working towards their personal goals and finding success. From losing 100lbs to breaking world records, you will be inspired.

I can't promise you'll break a world record or hit a new PR, but with the resources presented in this book and online course content, you'll be well on your way to swimming with more efficiency and greater confidence in the water.

I Swam Everyday for 30 Days

For one month, I challenged myself to swim every single day! No matter how tired I felt, or what my schedule looked like, I committed to swimming over 100,000 meters in just 30 days!

After 30 days of swimming, I successfully swam over 110,000 meters and raised thousands of dollars for the Movember Foundation. It was incredible to accomplish this goal, and it felt even sweeter because I had failed to do so the year prior. You see, I tried to swim 100,000 meters just 12 months earlier and fell short.

Failure is something we all experience at some point. It's nothing to be ashamed of. If anything, it should be embraced. Regardless of how you fail, or what you fail in, what's most important is what you do next! Success is not final; failure is not fatal. It's the courage to continue that counts.

In the following year of that failure, with a renewed motivation to hit 100,000 meters, I made a plan! I would swim every single day. No excuses! I needed to average at least 4,000 yards per day! That's about 3.5 kilometers or 2.2 Miles. Some days, I swam twice, changing up my workouts for variety's sake and to reduce the stress on my body.

Rather than swim continuously for 4,000 yards every session, I broke it up. I wrote out my workouts the day before using the MySwimPro app and loaded the workout onto my watch at the pool before each session! I followed a structured workout routine to stay on track and keep myself accountable to swimming the full distance.

I've never appreciated having a coach on my wrist as much as I did during this challenge because some days I really wanted to get out of the water early, but I had my coach pushing me to complete the next set! Swimming every single day was a new experience for me! Normally, I swim three times per week and mix in a dryland routine three or four times per week out of the water.

Even in college, we would only swim six days per week and have one day off to recover. So this challenge was definitely uncharted waters. Pun intended! You might be wondering what happens to your body when you swim every day with no days off!

Do you grow gills? Do your arms fall off?

While I didn't grow any gills (at least that I know of), I did develop an incredible feel of the water. The more time you spend in the water, the more refined this feel becomes. As soon as you stop swimming, you start to lose this feel of the water. And, the longer you're away from the water, the longer it will take for you to get that feel back.

Because I was swimming every day and averaged less than

24 hours between every swim, I felt an incredible connection to the water by the end of the month. Beyond feeling stronger in the water, I also experienced tons of health benefits. During these 30 days, my vital lung capacity improved, my average resting heart rate dropped, and I also got faster!

My average swimming pace dropped about 10% by the end of the month. I would find myself swimming freestyle with paddles at 1:10 pace per 100 yards easily. I could probably hold that pace for a few thousand yards continuously if I needed to. I was able to swim faster with less energy just by improving my feel of the water and developing a more robust aerobic capacity.

The endorphins were an added bonus, too. I always left the pool with a smile on my face! If you have not experienced the joy of swimming every day, I highly recommend it. Even if it's just for a week. The beauty of swimming is that you can do it at any age, unlike other sports that are high impact.

Swimming every day helped me develop a routine, disconnect from the daily grind, and build my character and mental confidence. But it also helped me make an impact on the world around me. As part of my challenge, I raised over a thousand dollars for the Movember foundation to support those men tackling prostate cancer, testicular cancer, mental health challenges, and suicide.

I shared my progress nearly every day with the MySwimPro community in our Facebook group and in the MySwimPro app. The community supported me and pushed me to reaching this goal. I also shared my progress on my personal social media accounts (@FaresKsebati), and I saw amazing support there as well.

When I first tried to swim 100,000 meters in 30 days, I failed. The following year, I learned from that experience, made the necessary changes, and I finally did it. Remember, whenever you think you've failed, reframe it as an opportunity to learn, grow and do better next time.

How I Swam From Asia to Europe

The Bosphorus is a narrow, natural straight that separates the continents of Asia and Europe!

It stretches 30 Kilometers and unites the Black Sea with the Sea of Marmara. The Bosphorus is the lifeblood of Istanbul, and every year for the last three decades, thousands of swimmers from around the world travel to Turkey to swim from one continent to the other. I successfully completed this exhilarating open water race in 2019 and thrilled to share what that experience was like!

The Bosphorus is one of the busiest waterways in the world, due to its strategic importance connecting The East and West. The city of Istanbul is home to over 15 Million residents and has been the capital city of three empires: Roman, Byzantine and Ottoman! The city, which was called Second Rome and New Rome at the beginning of the Modern Age, was later called "Byzantium" and Constantinople in later periods. These empires each left their incredible landmarks on the city's skyline.

Swimming in the Bosphorus, you can see countless palaces, mosques, churches, and monuments that mark Istanbul's rich history and culture. Every year, 2.5 thousand swimmers from around the world travel to Istanbul to compete in the annual Cross Continental Swim.

The race covers 6.5 kilometers of the Bosphorus in the heart of Istanbul. On the morning of the race, the straight completely shuts down for three hours. Just enough time to clear all the ferries, yachts, and ships for the moment I had anticipated for months. Tens of thousands of spectators line the Bosphorus on both the Asian and European sides to see a truly spectacular sight.

No where else will you see one of the busiest shipping channels in the world shut down so swimmers can race across it. The backdrop of Istanbul's magnificent Mosques, castles, and rich history adds a unique flavor to this one-of-a-kind spectacle.

All of the swimmers load onto two massive ships on the European side before being transported to the starting dock in

Asia. Onboard the ship, you can feel everyone's energy and excitement. Once we leave the dock, there's no turning back! We wear nothing but our swimsuits, goggles, caps, and tracking bracelets.

The ships are divided by age-group, and after a 15-minute cruise up the Bosphorus, we dock at the starting point. A starting platform is built in a matter of minutes. It's almost time for the race to begin! The anticipation is growing. Everyone on the boat is ready to go. The water is calm, but not for long. The event staff gives the final ok, then the gun goes off!

The first wave of swimmers dives into the vibrant, blue waters of the Bosphorus. The older swimmers began their journey back to Europe first while I waited patiently alongside 1,200 other swimmers. Within the first 30 seconds, over 500 swimmers have already started racing. I don't recall being nervous, I was more excited than anything.

What was once a vision of swimming between two continents was about to become a reality. In times like these, all your senses are firing. After a few minutes, most of the swimmers had entered the water, and finally, it was my turn to take the plunge. I walked to the edge of the starting platform, looked out at the nearly two thousand swimmers scattered across the Bosphorus, and dove in!

From afar, we looked like thousands of piranhas nipping at the surface. I felt strong, the water was cool, and I knew my sense of direction. Within a couple of minutes, I passed under the first bridge. The Fatih Sultan Mehmet bridge carries over 150,000 cars between Asia and Europe every day. I could barely believe I was swimming underneath it, and I couldn't help but swim a few strokes of backstroke to gaze up at this 8-lane suspension bridge. One of the largest in the world.

Moving past the first bridge, it became clear where the current was strongest. Veterans of this swim advise following the cool water flowing from the Black sea for the fastest swim. If you can catch the cold water, usually right in the middle of the straight, you'll be able to swim nearly twice as fast! If you miss the current and swim off to the side, you may get sucked into a negative draft on the shoreline and go practically nowhere. Sure enough, I found what I thought was the cold current and got into rhythm.

I felt strong, and the view was magnificent. The sight of Istanbul's architecture from the middle of the Bosphorus was something out of an epic film. Every breath I took gave me a new perspective of the horizon. Although I was one of the last swimmers to leave the starting platform, I wasn't concerned because I knew the final race time was based on my timing chip and not when the first swimmer entered the water.

I used this to my advantage, and over the next 30 minutes proceeded to pass approximately two thousand swimmers by the time I reached the second bridge near the finish. As I approached the finish, the current intensified. It was so strong, I felt like I was flying. I've never experienced anything like it.

The current is so powerful, in fact, that a series of safety boats position themselves just past the finishing platform to catch swimmers who get swept past the finish line. This happens to a couple dozen swimmers every year, and knowing this, I made sure to position myself accordingly for a strong finish.

As I neared the platform, I could see and hear thousands of spectators from the bleachers and shoreline. There were drones, helicopters, and fans at the park cheering for all of us to finish. I took my final few strokes into the platform, and climbed out.

I did it!

I swam from Asia to Europe! I was a cross continental swimmer, and it was an amazing experience. I placed third in my age group with a final time of 53 minutes and 36 seconds, and I was the fastest swimmer from the United States across all age-groups. I averaged 48 seconds per 100 meters. For context, the world record in the 100-meter freestyle is 46 seconds (set in a pool), meaning I swam at nearly world record pace for almost an hour.

This isn't to say how fast I am, but it's a testament to how strong the water's current is in the Bosphorus. Most swimmers take anywhere from 60 to 90 minutes to complete the swim. The record time for this swim was set in 2006 at 39 minutes, or 36 seconds per 100 meters.

The race is followed by a televised awards ceremony hosted by members of the local government. Family and friends gather to watch and congratulate each other on completing the cross continental swim! If you're considering this race, I highly recommend it! It's absolutely incredible.

The swim is well-organized, the views are magnificent, and the city of Istanbul is amazing! With international participants from over 50 countries, many travelers, including myself, take the opportunity to explore the beautiful city of Istanbul before and after the race.

Istanbul is one of the most popular tourist destinations in

the world, with a mesmerizing culture, delicious food, and a breathtaking skyline. I spent the week after the race exploring the city with my parents, and it was truly a once in a lifetime experience.

Thank you for joining me on this journey swimming from Asia to Europe. A video version of this short story is available to view in the online course material, so be sure to check it out and get the popcorn ready!

My First Triathlon

I was first introduced to the sport of triathlon when I watched the 2000 Olympic Games in Sydney, Australia. I was intrigued by how much training it took for these athletes to be highly competitive at three different sports. I remember watching highlight reels that showed how these athletes were training up to eight hours per day in pursuit of their Olympic dream!

At the time, I was in elementary school and could barely handle being in school for eight hours so the thought of doing anything like that seemed crazy. Little did I know that less than two decades later I would not only participate in triathlon but also coach triathletes. I even took it to another level and got certified as a USA Triathlon coach!

Over the last decade or so, I've had the unique opportunity to meet with hundreds if not thousands of triathletes. What I find the most fascinating is just how different everyone's background is coming into the sport. Some triathletes have never competed in anything their entire life, while others are former collegiate athletes. While the sport does attract a more competitive, Type-A personality, I personally know dozens of people who ascended to multiple Ironman's from very humble beginnings.

This is what I found most inspiring about the sport of triathlon. Similar to swimming, where you really don't need much background to get started, I found that triathlon offered a similar path to improvement. If you are consistent, seek out the right information, and work hard, you'll see initial progress almost right away.

I didn't really understand this until I finished swimming in college and moved onto the "real world" post university. It wasn't until I started coaching masters swimming that I started to truly realize just how different the motivations and goals triathletes had compared to fitness swimmers.

What I realized is that the triathletes I was working with had very little swimming or training knowledge. They were already training anywhere from 10-15 hours per week outside of the water and highly engaged with their workout regime. They came to me, their coach, often with fear, anxiety, and confusion around how to actually prepare for the swimming portion of a triathlon.

I did my best to research the specific differences between training for pool swimming and preparing for an open water race. I looked deeper into the differences between open water swimming and the first leg of a triathlon from a technique perspective. I also learned how the best athletes conserve energy during the swim portion of the race as well as the mental element of preparing for longer half-ironman and full ironman triathlon distances.

After weeks and months of working with triathletes on their specific goals, we were making progress, but I still felt like something was missing. Despite having a strong foundation in both pool and open water swimming, I felt compelled to actually experience a triathlon for myself. I was motivated to sign up for a race for a number of reasons.

Firstly, I had never done a triathlon and it seemed like something to experience for myself. Secondly, I was watching so many videos and reading numerous articles that I figured I must know enough to make this happen. Finally, I was surrounded by people who were preparing for specific races, and I wanted to fully experience this with them and see what it's like for myself.

In April, I signed up for a Sprint triathlon on Belle Isle, a beautiful island that sits in the middle of the Detroit River between the United States and Canada. The race was in June, and I knew that I was "in shape" enough to participate but wasn't sure just how taxing each of the three disciplines would be on my body. This sprint triathlon consisted of a 500 meter swim, 20 km bike ride, and finished with a 5km run.

At the time, I was fresh off my college swimming days and the thought of swimming 500 meters in open water seemed more like a warmup than an actual endurance race. For about two months, I picked up my weekly cycling distance and added running to my weight lifting routine out of the water. I felt aerobically fit and ready to take on my first sprint triathlon.

Looking back now, I find it comical how I arrived at the event on race morning. At the time, I was living in an apartment in downtown Detroit, and I didn't have a bike rack on my car or any way to get to the island with my bike. I figured it'd be easier to just ride my bike to the race course and figure it out when I arrive. This was my first mistake and what I learned to be a major component of these types of races.

Preparation is crucial, and it has more to do than just training. Your gear setup, nutrition, race plan, and execution all need to be rehearsed ahead of time. I'm someone who can think on their feet and doesn't get anxious very easily. I learned that this is a false sense of confidence that doesn't shield you from being fully mentally and physically prepared for an event like this.

I arrived to the transition area exhausted after biking 7km from my apartment with my race bag stuffed with my wetsuit, water bottles, snacks, and clothes. 7km felt like a lot more than it needed to ride on the pothole filled roads of Detroit with 10kg on my back at 6am. Regardless of how tired my legs were, I was not phased. I had no benchmark to compare myself to and was there to have fun and take in the full experience.

Luckily, the weather was fantastic, and it was all sunny skies, and smiles all around on the beach before the water race started. I was surprised and happy to see so many familiar faces on the beach. I was pumped to get started and patiently awaited my heat to be called into the water.

The water temperature was a crisp 18° Celsius (about 65° Fahrenheit) and felt pretty calm with my wetsuit on. When the horn sounded, we were off. I immediately remember just how fast everyone was swimming. I arrogantly thought I would be body lengths ahead of everyone within the first 50 to 100 meters. I was dead wrong!

If I could guess the split time of my first 50 meters, it would probably be less than 35 seconds. Despite this early speed, I was sandwiched between at least five or six other guys up until around 100-150 meters. I started to separate myself from the field just slightly, and as I imagined, I finished the swimming portion ahead of all the other participants.

At that moment, I thought I had conserved a lot of my energy on the swim. I felt strong with my technique and confident knowing I had just crushed the entire field in my first ever triathlon race. Boy was I wrong. Dead wrong!

Unfortunately, I was comparing that specific effort level to how much effort I exert in a sprint race in the pool. The first leg of a triathlon is completely different than racing a 100 meter breaststroke. In the pool, the goal is to expend 100% of your effort over the course of the race. In open water, and specifically in triathlon, I learned that even just swimming "easy" is not easy enough.

When I exited the water and ran over to the transition area, I felt calm and collected. I was still in the lead leaving T1 and then started the bike course. Two laps around the island equaled 20 km. Let's go!

As you can imagine, it wasn't long before all the other athletes in my heat started passing me on the bike course. It must have been less than two minutes before I was eventually passed by a dozen or so other athletes from my heat. My goal was never to win anything or care about my time in this race, but the adrenaline of the moment will always push you harder.

I tried to hold a strong pace on the bike, but I had put too much energy into the swim and my legs started to feel heavy. On top of that, I'm probably the weakest on the bike of all three disciplines. After about 10 minutes, I settled into my groove and just acknowledged the fact that I would be passed by biker after biker.

The other athletes sounded like bees zipping by every time they passed me, so I just tried to stay out of their way. It felt like driving on the freeway going the speed limit and everyone is dodging you going 15-20 kph over the limit. I just kept my course and did my thing.

When I got off the bike just before entering T2, my legs were completely jello. I had practiced a few brick workouts, where I would combine a bike, then go for a short run afterwards imme-diately after, but this feeling was something else entirely. I started the final leg of the race with a slow jogging pace, and was eventually able to finish the 5k run in about 24 minutes. I was relatively happy with that split because I had trained to hold that pace in the weeks leading up to the race.

When I crossed the finish line, I was so relieved. My body felt destroyed and excited at the same time. I was pumped to have accomplished something new, and I was grateful to be in the physical health to take something like this on. It was definitely a learning experience that I used as a launchpad to not only do more triathlon races in the future but also apply all these experiences to the athletes I coach.

Just like swimming, triathlon teaches you about perseverance, consistency, and work ethic. You don't have to take on Kona to be a triathlete just like you don't have to swim the English Channel to be a swimmer. What's most important is that you enjoy the experience.

Starting MySwimPro, Inc.

I learned how to swim when I was 5 years old. This was a privilege that my siblings and I had growing up in a waterfront community where it was the norm to learn how to swim at a young age. Surprisingly enough, my parents did not have this opportunity to learn how to swim growing up and were not confident in the water.

Swimming is a life skill, and this is how the sport starts for many who are lucky enough to learn how to swim at a young age. Most of my childhood friends learned how to swim in group lessons or private instruction. I completed all of the summer swim lessons, and I recall my mom saying "there was nothing left to sign you up for except for the swim team!"

Sure enough, my older brother and I joined the swim team, and we were terrible. I was 8 years old in my first summer league swim season, and while I don't remember very much about it, I knew I looked forward to going to the local park everyday to swim outside under the sun.

Fast forward about a decade, and I quickly became one of the best swimmers in the summer league but was still amazed at just how fast some of the other swimmers could swim. They made it look so easy, and I soon learned that these swimmers were training year-round at local USA club teams.

Growing up through the summer league, I became intrigued at how to optimize my own performance and learn from the faster swimmers. I went through high school and college with this self-coaching mindset.

When I was 17, it was an easy transition from swimmer to coach, because I was always looking at the sport through that lens. It wasn't until I finished college swimming and started coaching masters swimming that I realized how broken the adult fitness swimming model was.

It became clear that most adult fitness swimmers had almost zero swimming knowledge. A decent handful learned how to swim in a structured environment like I did, and a few even swam on a swim team growing up, but the vast majority were completely lost when it came to writing workouts or coming up with a plan to achieve a specific goal.

This is where the idea for MySwimPro was born. How could I merge my coaching knowledge with my entrepreneurial intuition? In addition to coaching swimming, I was working for a venture-backed technology startup in downtown Detroit. Prior to that, I had worked at several other high growth early stage companies and dabbled with projects on the side as well.

I've always been very entrepreneurial, but never thought I would build a company related to swimming. That is, until one day a swimmer in my masters group specifically asked me for a training program to follow while she traveled out of town for work. It seemed easy enough, but when she offered to pay me for the plan, a few more wheels started turning.

While I'd love to say this was the singular lightbulb moment for launching MySwimPro, that wouldn't give appropriate credit to the numerous other "a-ha" moments I had that year. It was 2014, and the boom of personal fitness apps was just beginning. Several apps like MyFitnessPal, MapMyRun, and Strava were starting to gain significant traction, yet there was no app for swimmers.

After more research, speaking with adult fitness swimmers, and acknowledging my unique understanding of the market, I decided to take action and make something happen! I wanted to validate that this was an idea worthy of pursuing, so I put together a mockup of what the app might look like, and purchased the domain MySwimPal.com.

Many people don't know this, but the initial idea for MySwimPro was MySwimPal. I set up a twitter account (@MySwimPal) and started sending traffic to the url to get people to put in their email to download an app that did not yet exist. After a few weeks, I had over 200 emails entered, and these swimmers served as my initial customer discovery.

Many of the initial conversations with swimmers who entered their email on my landing page reinforced my hypothesis. Nearly all of the swimmers I spoke with clearly articulated their struggle with writing workouts and training plans and improving their technique. That's exactly the problem MySwimPro was launched to solve, and we continue to work towards this every single day.

Fast forward a few years, and MySwimPro has grown to become an international community of swimmers with a globally distributed team! We are at the forefront of the swimming industry with our award-winning app, and we produce media content daily that educates, inspires, and entertains the next generation of swimmers.

We believe that everyone is one day away from achieving

their gold medal moment and we exist to empower people to achieve their dreams. We're all about empowering human potential for swimmers of all levels. In 2019, I was fortunate to give a TEDx talk titled **Idea to App of the Year**. It's the Cliff Notes version of how MySwimPro went from an idea to an award winning app with global impact.

My TEDx talk will be linked in the supplemental online companion course, and you can also watch it hosted on my YouTube channel. On my channel, I also share a behind-the-scenes look at what it's like to build a global technology and media company.

For everyone who joins the supplemental online companion course, I'll be offering a deep discount to our subscription plans for all new members. All this information is available at *swimlikeapro.org*.

Launching World Swim Day

World Swim Day is an international holiday that promotes living a healthy lifestyle through swimming and raises aware-ness for the importance of water safety. There are over 100 million fitness swimmers in the world, and yet there are over 4 billion people who do not know how to swim.

World Swim Day was actually born out of a marketing meeting at MySwimPro Inc. in 2018. At the time, I had a weekly marketing strategy meeting with our then Marketing Director, Paige Walters. We were brainstorming ways to bring attention to the sport of swimming when I asked when World Swim Day was.

After a few quick google searches, we realized there was no World Swim Day. How could this be? How is there not an international day for one of the most participated in forms of physical activity in the world?

As an entrepreneur, you must live in the future and build what's missing. I believe this deep down and decided to take action. That same day, I acquired the domain addresses worldswimday.com and worldswimday.org, and we started brainstorming what World Swim Day would look like!

World Swim Day was initially conceived to increase participation in swimming and promote water safety inclusive of geography, language, and skills. In the first year, World Swim Day saw participation from swimmers in over 100 countries and funds were raised for three learn-to swim non-profit organizations.

In the following years, the event has grown to global sponsors, independently hosted meetups, and incredible stories shared on social media with the hashtag #WorldSwimDay. The goal is for World Swim Day to continue to inspire and empower people around the world to be active in the water, lead happier lives, and reflect on everything the sport has to offer.

You can learn more about supporting World Swim Day at worldswimday.org.

So where do you go from here?

It's been an incredible journey launching MySwimPro, World Swim Day, and now this book! I'm so thankful for the opportunity to serve a global community and give back to the sport I love so much.

Take every opportunity to enjoy and appreciate the water. The feeling of weightlessness we experience while swimming is unlike anything else we'll ever experience. This magical feeling is one of the many joys the sport of swimming offers humanity.

If you'd like to be a part of my swimming journey, you can

follow me on social media (@FaresKsebati). I'd love to connect with you! Tag me and use the hashtag,

#SwimLikeAPro

It would mean the world to me if you shared my book with anyone else you think it will help. You can also take a photo with the book and tag me on social media. I'd love to see all the amazing pools and beaches from around the world that our community swims in! I can't wait to share your amazing pictures with the swimming community!

The supplemental online companion course is another great way to stay connected and I will continue to add and update content to this website as time goes on. We also have a vibrant facebook group for the MySwimPro global community. This is a free group that will also be linked in the companion course.

I'm very active online and in that Facebook group, so I look forward to seeing you there. That group is amazing, and I guarantee you will be inspired by over 10,000 other swimmers from 100+ countries who are passionate about improving their swimming!

Thank you again! I'm looking forward to following your swimming journey for decades to come.

Happy swimming :)

APPENDICES

APPENDIX I: SWIMMING GLOSSARY

EVERY SPORT and activity has its own unique language. This "jargon" or specialized terminology associated with a particular sport or industry evolves over time. In swimming, it can feel like a different language entirely if you're not familiar with some basic terms and phrases.

This appendix section highlights some of the most common swimming terminology used in this book and in the real world. Please don't let these terms or any swimming lingo discourage you from reaching your full potential in the sport. A full swimming terms library is linked in the supplemental online companion course as well!

WORKOUT TERMS

- **Set:** Full workouts are broken up into sets. Sets are composed of four elements: The number of repetitions, distance to be swum, stroke type, and interval.

- **Interval:** Interval is a unit of measure for time. In traditional structured training systems, the total interval is composed of swim time plus rest time.
- **Zone:** Often referred to as "training zone" or "energy zone", this represents the perceived exertion level of a particular set in a workout. It can also correspond to a specific heart rate zone.
- **Repetition:** The number of reps in a set is the number of times you swim that distance inside of a single set. The singular form of repetitions is one "rep".
- **Set Group:** Also known as "Super Sets" in strength and conditioning, a Set Group is simply a collection of more than one set. Set groups can have multiple repetitions, so a Set Group with two repetitions means you perform all of the sets in that Set Group twice.

TECHNIQUE

- **Streamline:** Streamline is the fundamental body position in swimming and is used as a starting point for pushing off the wall or diving into the water. A good streamline starts with one hand over the other with the arms extended above the head. The goal is to minimize resistance from fingertips to toes.
- **SWOLF:** This is a metric used to measure swimming efficiency. SWOLF is calculated per-length as the sum

of the time it took you to swim the lap, and the number of strokes it took you to swim it normalized to a 25-meter pool. For example, if you swim 25 meters in 20 seconds and take 20 arms strokes (10 stroke cycles), your SWOLF score would be 40.

- **Open Turn:** A technique used to change direction at the wall. Primarily used in Breaststroke and Butterfly. This type of turn is initiated with both hands touching the wall simultaneously.
- **Flip Turn:** A somersault at the wall used to change direction. Primarily used in freestyle and backstroke.
- **Bilateral Breathing:** A technique used in freestyle in order to breathe on both the right and left sides. Usually every three or five arm strokes.
- **Distance Per Stroke (DPS):** The total distance traveled per arm stroke or stroke cycle. Typically a technique used to improve stroke length and overall efficiency. The fewer strokes you take per length, the higher your DPS.
- **Breakout Stroke:** The first stroke taken from a streamline position after pushing off the wall or diving in the water. The first stroke, and often the first few strokes, carries the most speed from momentum generated from wall or racing start.

TRAINING

- **Kick:** Making forward progress in the water without using your arms (legs only). You may use a kickboard to help keep your head above water, or you can hold a streamline on your back or stomach. Kick sets are meant to help you focus on improving your kick, so you can kick stronger during regular swimming.

- **Drill:** An exercise used to focus on a specific element of swimming technique. It's usually a modified version of a competition stroke like swimming Butterfly with only one arm, or swimming freestyle with your hands in a fist position.

- **Pull:** Swimming without the use of your legs. This can be done with or without equipment including a pull buoy, paddles, or a rubber tube around the ankles.

- **IM:** Short for "Individual Medley", a style of swimming that involves swimming all four major competitive strokes in the order of: Butterfly, Backstroke, Breaststroke, Freestyle. For example, a 100 IM would be 25 butterfly, 25 backstroke, 25 breaststroke, 25 freestyle.

- **Split:** The amount of time it takes to swim a specific distance, usually in reference to a singular repetition of a set or segment of a set or race.

- **Negative Split:** Swimming faster on the second half of an individual repetition, set, set group, or entire workout. This can also apply to an entire race distance.

- **Build:** Swimming a specific set, set group, or race in a way that you increase speed by the end of it. You can think of it as "Speeding up" within the specific segment.

- **Descend:** Swimming faster by time over the duration of a set or repetition. Descending splits over a series of repetitions is a common training methodology that is similar to building and negative split.

- **Ascend:** Swimming slower by time over the duration of a set or repetition.
- **Best Average:** Swimming as fast as possible, maintaining the same speed on every repetition within a set. Often corresponding to the "SP1" energy zone.
- **Aerobic Training:** An energy pathway which requires your cells to use oxygen. If you are training aerobically, the idea is that your cells will generally not need to enter anaerobic respiration to produce energy. These types of sets are lower intensity over a longer duration of time.
- **Anaerobic Training:** An energy pathway that does not require oxygen and is generally only used if oxygen is not available. If you are training anaerobically, the idea is that your cells will produce most of their energy using anaerobic respiration. These types of sets are high intensity, shorter durations that often produce lactic acid.

EQUIPMENT

- Fins
- Paddles
- Snorkel
- Pull Buoy
- Kick Board

These are the most common pieces of equipment that you'll see on the pool deck. In the supplemental online course, I share specific pieces of equipment to purchase in my *Swim Like A Pro Equipment Guide*. In this list, you'll find links of different products to purchase for swimmers of different skill levels and goals.

APPENDIX II: FREQUENTLY ASKED QUESTIONS

OVER THE LAST DECADE, I've had the incredible opportunity to field thousands of questions from swimmers all over the world. Oftentimes, there are a few core themes that these questions fall into. Some swimmers are focused on losing weight, while others are more concerned with dropping time. Many swimmers simply want to know how to get started with choosing a workout plan. In the supplemental online companion course, I made a specific video answering all of the questions below and more.

- How do I lose weight swimming?
- How many times per week should I swim?
- What equipment should I use?
- When should I use equipment?
- Why should I swim anything other than freestyle?
- How do I stop my legs from sinking?

- Should I do dryland before or after swimming?
- Can I swim while pregnant?
- How do I get ready for my first open water race?
- Do I need a swim coach?

I'll continue adding video responses to the most common questions swimmers have in the online course. You can join the online course at *swimlikeapro.org*, I'll be creating new videos directly responding to questions from the community. I'm looking forward to answering your questions!

ABOUT MYSWIMPRO

MYSWIMPRO IS a technology and media company founded in 2015 to help swimmers improve their performance and health. The company developed the MySwimPro mobile app, which offers personalized training plans including swim and dryland workouts. In 2019, the app passed 1 million downloads and has been translated into 9 languages.

MySwimPro was named by Apple as the Best App of the Year for the Apple Watch in 2016 and has been featured in international publications like Sports Illustrated. The app has a global community of members in over 180 countries. The team is 100% remote, led by its co-founder and CEO, Fares Ksebati.

TO LEARN MORE ABOUT MYSWIMPRO, GO TO:

myswimpro.com

ABOUT THE AUTHOR

FARES KSEBATI is an entrepreneur, swimmer, coach, and mentor, helping people turn their dreams into a reality. He has been featured by Apple, Forbes, and Men's Health. Fares is the Co-Founder of MySwimPro, World Swim Day, and multiple business ventures that have impacted millions of people around the world.

Fares is an avid world traveler and keynote speaker. He is a Bosphorus Cross-continental swimmer, and three time U.S.

Masters Swimming individual national champion. His goal is to inspire and empower others to take action on their dreams. He advocates for a growth mindset and continuous self-improvement! Follow his journey on social media @FaresKsebati.

TO LEARN MORE ABOUT FARES, GO TO:

www.faresksebati.com

SWIM LIKE A PRO ONLINE VIDEO COURSE

To help guide your swimming journey, I created an online video course that includes swim drills, workouts, links to additional video content and an exclusive Q&A section that will grow over time. I truly believe that the best way to learn something is through multiple touch points.

This is your first step towards success with this book as I have created a unique video for each chapter. You'll be able to see and hear my explanation for each concept and stroke technique in this book. Seeing a visual representation of each concept can make all the difference in how fast you make progress, so I highly recommend you join the online course.

You can get started right away by visiting swimlikeapro.org or by opening the camera app on your phone. Hold your phone over the QR code below. Your phone will automatically direct you to the website where you can follow the instructions to unlock all the video content.

The online course has bonus video sections, a swim workout

template, and interviews with swimmers who have lost weight, completed Ironmans, and even won Olympic Medals! While the online video course is not required, I encourage you to check it out.

Visit the link below to unlock access to the full Swim Like A Pro experience:

ONLINE COURSE

SCAN THE CODE

TO SWIM LIKE A PRO

VIDEO LIBRARY

WORKOUTS

Q&A

GET CUSTOM STROKE ANALYSIS & COACHING

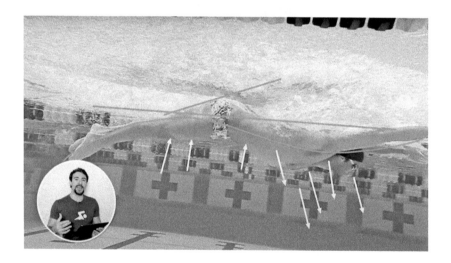

WOULD you like me to analyze your stroke technique?

Swimming with proper technique is critical to swimming faster and reaching your full potential! I can analyze your stroke technique by providing detailed audio and visual feedback. I will provide a comprehensive analysis of your stroke, mark the footage with real-time telestration, and offer corrective feedback and drill recommendations.

All you need to do is upload your video online, choose the analysis & coaching package on the same website as the Swim Like A Pro online course, and I'll take care of the rest! I can analyze all four competitive strokes, starts, turns, drills, and even dryland training. No special equipment required. We can even set up a time for a video call to discuss your technique and a strategy to help you reach your goals!

ACKNOWLEDGMENTS

Thank you, first and foremost, to the MySwimPro global community who have motivated and supported me through the years. Thank YOU for reading this book, sharing it with your friends and being a part of the swimming family! I've seen the impact swimming has had on so many people's lives, and I'm so humbled to be a small part of these success stories. I'm so thankful to be a part of a community that is supportive and pushes me to be the best version of myself. I will continue to serve you through the work that I do.

I'd like to give a huge shout out to my family. When my parents moved to the United States, they signed my brother and I up for swim lessons to learn how to swim, an opportunity they didn't have growing up in Damascus, Syria. I fell in love with the water and continue to swim to this day because of that. I turned this passion for swimming into a business that now helps people all over the world improve their performance and health and I'm thankful for my family's continued encouragement. To my parents, I love you! To my brother and sister, I love you!

Another important group of people I'd like to thank are all the swim coaches I've had along the way. From my summer league, high school, and club team, thank you to: Bill Thomson, Eric Gunderson, John Fodell, Elizabeth Nelson, Ryan Wheaton, Joe Ryan, Scott MacDonald, and many more for pushing me to do my best in and out of the water.

Huge shout out to my collegiate swim team and coaches, Sean Peters and Bryce Pitters. A huge thank you to the Wayne State University swim team for taking me in and allowing me to represent my school in swimming! I'm so lucky to have had this opportunity and make life-long friends. It was also an incredible experience to learn more about the sport and take my own swimming to the next level!

Thank you to the MySwimPro team, our ambassadors, advisors, and investors. Thank you to my co-founders of MySwim-Pro, Adam Oxner and Michael Allon, for taking a leap of faith on me and my crazy ideas. Thank you to our team: Benjamin Hendricks, Paige Walters, Arthur Shi, Max Bilan, Charlie Brown, Cenk Arioz, Lorenza Padilla, Carol Caldas, Daniel Plantamura, Taylor Holmes and Steve Dalal. Thank you to our advisors: Peter Vanderkaay, Todd Sullivan, Mitch Thrower, and many more mentors in the startup and swimming community.

A few more acknowledgements are in order! The original Di team of Alex Bordyukov, Valentino Smith, and Casey Browning! We trained together over the years and created a legendary hype video. Thank you to Michigan Masters swimming and a huge shout out to my swim teammates at Wayne State University and our epic Harlem Shake dance video that went viral! Thank you also to the masters swim group at the Detroit Athletic Club!

Thank you to Lauren Johnson for helping me make this book a reality. Thank you to everyone who agreed to help promote and share MySwimPro or Swim Like A Pro in some way, shape, or form, thank you! To all those who allowed me to speak at your events, come on podcasts, and video interviews, thank you!

To all who read this, here's to you and your future. I wish you the very best and happy swimming :)

Milton Keynes UK
Ingram Content Group UK Ltd.
UKHW051108021223
433446UK00010B/167